Shadows flee away

Shadows flee away
Selmeston Church
& Churchyard

by

Rodney Castleden & Ann Murray

- Blatchington Press -

Until the day break, and the shadows flee away,
turn, my beloved, and be thou like a roe or a young hart
upon the mountains of Bether.
King James Bible: *Song of Solomon 2: 17*

The first line appears on the memorial to Nellie Moore, who is buried in Selmeston churchyard (plot A09).

Cover image
Front: photograph of Selmeston churchyard by Ann Murray.

Published in 2020
by Blatchington Press
Rookery Cottage, Blatchington Hill,
Seaford, East Sussex BN25 2AJ
© Rodney Castleden & Ann Murray 2020

ISBN: 978-1-71669-394-6

~ Contents ~

~ Part Two ~
The Monumental Inscriptions   89

~

~ 1 ~

Acknowledgements & Introduction

Selmeston is one of five parishes in a joint benefice, the other parishes being Berwick, Alciston, Arlington and Wilmington. The benefice is ably run by the Rector of Berwick, the Revd Peter Blee. We are grateful to Peter for agreeing to let us undertake this survey of the inscriptions in his church and churchyard at Selmeston, and also for his positive and continuing support for the project. We also thank Selmeston's churchwarden, Mrs Janet Matthews, for her support and help in giving us access to the church's vestry, where we found, as at Berwick church, that some of the commemorative stone slabs lifted from the floor of the nave and chancel during the nineteenth restoration had been reused to make the vestry floor. It was particularly useful to be allowed to record the vestry inscriptions, which are not normally accessible to the public. Jeremy Shaw, a past churchwarden, helped us by supplying some background to the recent history of the parish and in particular the creation of the joint benefice.

The photographs were taken by Ann Murray and the line drawings were drawn by Rodney Castleden.

The Selmeston project had its beginnings in the Seaford Monumental Inscriptions Group's trial run on the inscriptions at St Peter's, East Blatchington. Ann and I joined the Group at that time. Then, when recording the East Blatchington inscriptions was completed, we moved on with the group to tackle the substantially larger churchyard at St Leonard's, Seaford. After that, the group decided to record the Seaford Town Cemetery. At that point, Ann and I decided to part company with the Group; the Town Cemetery, founded at the end of the nineteenth century, held less historical interest for us.

After a short break from recording monumental inscriptions, Ann and I, just the two of us, decided to record the inscriptions at St Andrew's, Bishopstone. Because we were instinctively working to similar standards of accuracy, we found that working together as a pair was easier, more congenial and more productive than working within a larger group with disparate interests.

While we were working at Bishopstone, we were approached by the Revd Daniel Merceron, who was at that time the Rector of Alfriston. He had heard from the East Blatchington rector, the Revd Andrew Mayes, that Ann and I had recorded both of Andrew's churches, East Blatchington and Bishopstone being a two-parish joint benefice under his care, and Daniel wondered if we would be ready to record the inscriptions at his own church, St Andrew's, Alfriston. We were very ready to agree to this as our next project because of the historical importance of both the village and its church, but some confusion followed. Daniel left Alfriston for a post elsewhere and, now rectorless, the Alfriston churchwardens decided that they did not want us to continue. At that point, Crispin Freeman, Treasurer to the Berwick PCC, heard that our project had been beached, and wondered if we would be ready to turn our attentions to nearby Berwick church instead. A discussion with the Rector of Berwick, the Revd Peter Blee, followed, and he warmly welcomed our offer to record the inscriptions at Berwick.

The five sets of inscriptions - East Blatchington, Seaford, Bishopstone, Berwick and Selmeston - have all been published by Blatchington Press.[1] The layout of each book follows the same pattern: an introduction, followed by plans of the church and churchyard to help readers locate the inscriptions. The churchyard is divided into sectors, each identified by a letter of the alphabet. Within each sector the graves and other monuments are numbered, so a particular inscription might be referenced G34. After the set of plans comes the full record of the inscriptions.

Each inscription is printed in a box to a common format, with the surname of the central personality, the focus of the inscription, in the top right hand corner for quick reference. The layout of the inscription is reproduced as closely as possible to the original, line for line, with spelling and punctuation faithfully recorded. The same fonts are used uniformly throughout: Verdana for the plot number (top left) and surname identifier (top right), and Garamond for the text of the inscription. Within the inscription, the name of the central figure is given in bold capitals, to give it prominence, regardless of the way it is shown on the gravestone, where it might be upper or lower case. This standardized presentation should make the books easier to use. Finally, at the end of the book there is an alphabetical index of surnames, in each case with the plot number attached. This is to enable readers pursuing family history to find their relatives as easily as possible.

This same format has been used in all five of the books produced so far. All are available as Blatchington Press books, either from me or from Lulu.com, except the East Blatchington and Seaford volumes. The Seaford Monumental Inscriptions Group decided they did not want their volumes to continue to be on sale. It is to be hoped that in time they will change their minds and that all of the books will become available.

The monumental inscriptions recorded in Part 2 have been read from the stones themselves, not taken from earlier publications; as far as we know the Selmeston inscriptions have not been collected before. The notes below the inscriptions are mainly about the design and condition of the monument, for recognition purposes, but also in some places include additional details where appropriate from the parish registers. The Selmeston Churchyard Register for the years 1813-1994 is kept in the church vestry, while the Old Burial Register covering the period from 1667 to 1813 is in The Keep at Falmer. Ann Murray collected the relevant information from both and, where we thought it was useful, it has been incorporated in the notes, in each case referenced with the letters 'PR', for Parish Register. Some of the inscriptions have been damaged by weathering, and the parish registers are useful in supplying ambiguous or even missing lettering. In some instances, where the inscription is legible, differences emerge between the monument and the paper record; for those we have simply noted the two versions, leaving it to the reader to decide which is the more reliable.

Sir Egerton Brydges' *Topographical Miscellanies* can be useful in supplying inscriptions that existed and were legible in 1792. The book includes such inscriptions at Firle, Alciston, Berwick and Arlington, but unfortunately none for Selmeston.

Part One of the book is an introduction to the history of the church and churchyard. It is intended as background and should not be taken as an attempt at a comprehensive history. Instead the focus is on specific points and issues of interest. Quite a lot of archaeological research has been carried out at Selmeston, but published in technical language in academic journals that on the whole are inaccessible to general readers. This project seemed a good opportunity to bring some interesting and curious features of Selmeston's past to a more general readership. Selmeston's history is full of interest and its pre-Conquest prehistory is in its way quite remarkable. The site of the churchyard has been a focal point in the landscape for a very long time, since long before the church itself was built.

Selmeston is a village that has changed little in the last 200 years, so it may be useful to set the scene with the Sussex historian Thomas Horsfield's description of the locality as it was in the early 1830s.[2]

The small parish of Selmeston, which contains only 1,140 acres, is about seven miles east of Lewes, and is bounded on the north by Ripe and

Chalvington; on the west by Firle; on the east and south by Arlington, Berwick, and Alciston; whilst the new Eastbourne turnpike road runs along its southern boundary. The village had, in 1831, a population of 189 only. It is near the foot of the South Downs, north-eastward of the point known as Firle Beacon. The situation is high, and the prospect agreeable.

The ancient and respectable family of Caldecott resided for many years at Sherrington, in this parish,[3] which is now possessed by the Misses Mary Ann and Sarah Ann Skinner, who, with Mr Skinner, reside here, and are also the owners of the manor of Sherrington, which is a small manor comprising freehold property only, and has constantly descended with the Sherrington estate.[4]

The family name of Rochester, which afterwards removed to Jevington, appears also, from the monumental inscriptions in the chancel, to have been, at an early period, of considerable note here. [5]

Mays, in this parish, was formerly the seat of the well known family of Nutt, of which the notorious Sir Thomas Nutt was a member.[6] Mr Fuller, the late proprietor and present tenant, erected a substantial and regular edifice, a few years since, on the scite of the old mansion. Together with the manor of Ludlay, it is now the possession of Viscount Gage.

The principal landowners are Lord Viscount Gage and the Misses Skinner: the former is the proprietor of Mays and Tilton, and the latter of Sherrington.

The manor is placed in Doomsday in the hundred of Wandelmestrei. This manor, together with that of Sidenore, are said to have been held, in the Saxon times, as allodial land.[7] When, however, the Earl of Moreton became possessor of the rape [of Pevensey], those estates were subject to him as lord paramount. When Doomsday was compiled, the two manors were rated at four hides and a half; the arable was seven plough lands. A church, a priest, and five ministers, were maintained on these possessions. In 23rd Edward I, Roger Lewknor held this manor of the king. It continued in the possession of the Lewknors till 44th Elizabeth, when it seems to have passed to John Wood. In 1700, it was the property of Robert Rochester, gent, whose son Robert devised this manor, with Wannock in Jevington, to Olive Eversfield, (his wife's sister, and sister to Sir Charles Eversfield, Bart.) for life, with the *remainder to the Revd John Rideout, in tail male, and the remainder to Charles Gilbert, gent.*

The benefice is an undischarged vicarage in the deanery of Pevensey and diocese of Chichester. The Prebendary of Heathfield is patron of the living. Its yearly value is stated by Ecton to be £44. 15s. 7d., and the tenths to be 10s 7d. The Rev. H. Latham is the present encumbent. The rectory of Selmeston is holden of the manor of Wilmington, by the yearly rent of 6s 8d. It was the property of the Revd Sefton, who alienated it, in 1705, to John Fuller, Esq, from whom it has descended to the present possessor, A. E. Fuller, Esq. The church is small and ancient, and consists of a nave, chancel and south aisle. There are a few monumental inscriptions worth recording. . . Selmeston Fair, for sheep, cattle, &c., is held on the 19th of September.

A curious ring of gold and silver inmixed, having rude figures of the Trinity engraved thereon, was found here some time ago, and is in the cabinet of Mr C. Ade of Milton.

The registers commence in 1677 only, the former register having been lost.

~

RC & AM

~ Part One ~

Church & Churchyard a Long History

~

~ 2~

Very early beginnings

Selmeston today: 'no Bustle at all'

Selmeston is a small linear village, mainly limited to a single street, *The* Street, an address once to be found in many English villages. Most of its houses front this very nearly straight country lane, with mature hedgerows and trees down both sides, conserving its strong rural character. This is a piece of Wealden countryside where buildings seem incidental, indeed almost intrusive.

The southern end of the village is marked by The Street's junction with the main road through the area, the busy A27, which has been the focus of a small amount of commercial development, with a petrol station and a thriving pub, the Barley Mow. Halfway along the Street two tracks join it: one, to the west, is the drive to Sherrington Manor, the other, to the east, is the access road to The Green House. To the north, there is a dwindling straggle of houses and cottages as The Street makes its gradual and gentle descent into the Vale of Sussex, the Low Weald.

Selmeston has always been a quiet place. Eighteenth century elections were generally noisy, boisterous affairs. Reports to the Pelhams, a family of political grandees, on electioneering in 1741 commented on the activities of political agents across the country. Here at Selmeston, as might be expected, there was very little happening. The report on this area stated that 'Selmeston Fair was very quiet. There was no Bustle at all. Mr Sergison was not there.' Mr Sergison was one of the parliamentary candidates.

Today, there is still no bustle. Only 160 people live in the parish as a whole, which means there has been little change since the first census was taken over 200 years ago. On the other hand the lifestyle of the residents has changed enormously. For many centuries nearly everyone in the parish was involved in one way or another with agriculture, but today only 12% of the residents are involved in farming. Of the remainder, some are commuters, some retired, while the rest work from home.

The southern part of the parish is on the Lower Greensand, which forms a broad low plateau, while the north is on the Weald Clay, which is lower still. The landscape is very subdued and undulating, typical of the Vale of Sussex. Selmeston village is halfway between the alluvial floodplains of Glynde Reach to the west and the Cuckmere to the east. The Street precisely follows the low watershed that separates the catchment areas of the Ouse and the Cuckmere.

The most noticeable feature of the churchyard is its unusual shape: not rectangular, nor even a straight-sided irregular polygon. It is round: not exactly circular, but nearly so. The modern churchyard has an odd kink on the south-east perimeter which interrupts the balloon shape, but the Tithe Map shows that in the early nineteenth century the eastern side was continuously smooth and rounded, making the churchyard much more nearly circular than it is today. The rounded shape is significant, in that it suggests a pre-Conquest origin, perhaps in the Dark Ages, and perhaps earlier than that. The round enclosure surrounds an asymmetrical low knoll, a tilted knoll with a perimeter that is lower on the eastern side than the western.

The churchyard enclosure was there before the village street. We can tell this because the street respects it by bending round it. If the Street had been there first, the churchyard, like any other enclosure, would be set to one side. Not only does the Street go round the west side of the churchyard, the stretches to the north and south are on slightly different alignments. This could have arisen because the street approaching from the SSW was lined up on the church spire or whatever man-made structure stood on the site before the church was built. Either way, the relationship between churchyard and village street implies that the churchyard was there first. The segment of the Street approaching from the NNE may also have been oriented on the spire or whatever was there before it. These points together – the irregular rounded shape of the churchyard and the different alignments of the two segments of The Street – suggest an early origin for the churchyard, and whatever originally stood inside it.

The same is true for Slubby Lane, which gently skirts the southern edge of the churchyard as it leaves the village street before continuing to the east. If this lane is Romano-British in origin, as has been suggested, it implies that the churchyard existed before the Roman period.

This cursory look at the layout of Selmeston as it is today has already taken us to a different place and a different time, many centuries ago.

Stone age Selmeston

At one time sand was dug out of sandpits close to Selmeston Church. These are now disused. They have grown over and been softened by a cover of vegetation, but the deep hollows remain and are immediately recognizable as old quarries. There were some sandpits immediately to the north-northeast of the churchyard and a short distance to the east as well, a minute's walk along Slubby Lane, which leads to The Green House. The Tithe Map shows that there was already a small sandpit at the Slubby Lane site between the churchyard and Green House in 1840, but it was only when this sandpit was enlarged in the 1930s that prehistoric remains were recognized. There may have been earlier encounters with antiquity that went unrecognized: finds that were not seen for what they were. Excavation in 1933 revealed evidence that Mesolithic people had lived there, intermittently between 10,000 and 4,000 BC.[1]

Several Mesolithic pits or working hollows were found and in the hollows the remains of a cooking hearth, pot-boilers and some pit dwellings, together with over 130 flint microliths and many waste flakes.

The village of Selmeston is on the Lower Greensand escarpment. In the 1970s, on the same escarpment at Ditchling, 2,000 Mesolithic worked flints were found, in an area thirty metres square at the foot of Lodge Hill. A high percentage of the flints consisted of waste flakes. The small number of flint tools included several hammerstones.[2] The Greensand outcrop that runs right across Sussex seems to have attracted Mesolithic activity and settlement, though the hard evidence for settlement is elusive. Selmeston is a rare site in this respect, in that direct evidence of prehistoric settlements has survived there into modern times. We know for certain that there were houses at Selmeston, probably shaped like large wigwams, in the middle stone age.

After the time when Selmeston was inhabited by Mesolithic people it was deserted for a time, and the hollows in the land surface had almost filled up with wind-blown sand when Neolithic people visited the site and occupied one of the old working hollows. The presence of wind-blown sand suggests that there might have been land clearance on a significant scale on the Greensand outcrop in the late Mesolithic or early Neolithic. Only deforestation could have exposed the sand to wind erosion. The new people left behind evidence of their reoccupation in the form of hearths and fragments of their distinctive cord-impressed pottery. Mesolithic people did not make pottery, so in this respect the Neolithic settlers here were technologically more advanced. The use of pottery, as well as the domestication of plants and animals, marked them out as different, as new people with a new way of living.[3]

Selmeston sits on a low ridge with its crest just higher than 30 metres above sea level, running west-east and pointing towards the Cuckmere. This subdued landscape feature would have been attractive for settlement because it provided dry sites for huts, while at the same time being within easy reach of spring water.

A Mesolithic tranchet axe 7.2cm long was discovered in the back garden of the Old Vicarage. The axe compares well with the larger axe that Holloway found at the sandpit site. Holloway realised that the Mesolithic occupation site extended much further than originally thought, well beyond the confines of the large sandpit. He explored ten fields in Selmeston parish and across the parish boundary onto Berwick Common, adjacent to the east, and every one of them yielded Mesolithic flintwork. This broad low Greensand ridge was evidently a very popular place to live in the middle stone age.

Several more Mesolithic period sites are known at Selmeston. They can be summarized as follows;

Site B (at OS grid reference 513068), immediately south of Selmeston sandpit (Site A), yielded a heavy concentration of Mesolithic flintwork include two complete tranchet axes, a triangular core tool, micro-knife segments, scraper and cores.

Site C (at 513066) on Gault Clay, immediately south of site B, produced two large core hand-tools that were probably chisels.

Site D (at 520065) on Lower Greensand, three-quarters of a mile south-east of the sandpit, on Berwick Common yielded a heavy concentration of Mesolithic flintwork.

Site E (at 520063) and F (at 519062) on the Gault Clay, immediately south of site D, yielded small quantities of Mesolithic flintwork, mostly cores and flint flakes.

Site G on the Gault Clay (at 522069) yielded a small quantity of Mesolithic flint.

Site H (at 522069) produced a wide scatter of flints, cores and waste flakes.

Sites J (at 525054) and K (at 526056) on the Gault Clay produced a wide scatter of Mesolithic flints, including two petit tranchet arrowheads.

Site L (at 530056) on the Lower Greensand yielded half of a naturally perforated mace-head made of brown flint; it had been used as a hammer.

From these finds we can see that Selmeston was a significant Mesolithic occupation site. Until recently it has been assumed that Mesolithic settlement sites were only occupied seasonally, and that people were semi-nomadic, but some sites may have been occupied permanently, to judge from the solidity of the houses. Mesolithic material came to the surface in 1970 because new landowners ploughed to a greater depth than previous owners, who only dug to a depth of fifteen centimetres; shallow ploughing left prehistoric artefacts undisturbed.

After the Mesolithic, in about 4500 BC, came the Neolithic. In 1974 John Bell found an early Neolithic pot eroding out of the disused sandpit at 5125 0688. It came from the same site as the Mesolithic pit-dwellings excavated in 1933 by Clark, and close to the (post-Neolithic) Bronze Age ditch features located by the Curwens three years later. The site is on the edge of the Lower Greensand near its junction with the Gault Clay, so it is surrounded by springs. The abundance of springs close at hand may be the reason why people settled here repeatedly in the Mesolithic, Neolithic and Bronze Age.

An early Bronze Age barbed and tanged arrowhead was found on the site of the sandpit. This indicates that hunters crossed the sandpit site, as no other early Bronze Age finds have been made there. But the hunters must have lived not far away, as there was a Bronze Age burial ground in Millmans Mead, the field to the south of the church. There was also a middle Bronze Age barrow 500 metres west-southwest of the Selmeston Mesolithic site, and just to the west of the modern village. These burials show that people were living in the area in the Bronze Age.

Romano-British Selmeston

In 1955, Ivan Margary speculated that there might have been a Roman road running diagonally across the area, southwest to northeast, from Newhaven to the Dicker. He further speculated that this road crossed another Roman road close to Selmeston Church.[4] These two crossing roads are the village lane running southwest-northeast and now called The Street, and the bridleway south of the church and known as Slubby Lane, which runs east-west and would have joined Selmeston and Pevensey to the east. The continuation of this route, via the southern part of The Street, was along the line of the present A27 to connect Selmeston with Glynde to the west. These routes are perpetuated in map after map of 'Roman Sussex', but unfortunately there is little archaeological evidence to support Margary's theory.

In 1939, Ivan Margary published a detailed account of the route of a Roman road from Pevensey westwards to a river crossing at Glynde. He argued that the West Gate at Pevensey is one of the most imposing Roman remains in Sussex, and that although there must have been an important road leading away to the west from it no serious attempt to trace it had until then been attempted. In 1868, during the course of building work, distinct traces of the Roman road from Pevensey to Lewes were found at Polegate. This fixed one of the points along the route. Margary quoted *Downland Pathways* by Hadrian Allcroft for support for additional segments of the route: across the Cuckmere at Chilver Bridge, then westwards across Berwick Common to Selmeston Church. Mark Antony Lower supported this itinerary, a route from Pevensey via Polegate, Berwick Common and Glynde to Lewes.[5]

Margary skilfully used a charter of 1252 to confirm that this 'old way' across the landscape was sufficiently important and easy to identify in the middle ages as to be used as a boundary for a royal grant of free warren (to Peter of Savoy). The area granted was everything between the 'old way' from Pevensey to Glynde Bridge and the sea. In the charter, Selmeston is mentioned, as 'Sihalmeston'.[6]

In spite of the lack of evidence for the southwest-northeast road to Newhaven, there is some slight evidence of a Romano-British settlement in Selmeston. Many fragments of Roman pottery have been found and The Street, continuing south-westwards up to Bo-Peep, is a known Roman route onto the Downs.

Current thinking about the Roman road system still follows Ivan Margary's view. He argued convincingly for a Roman road leaving the west gate of Pevensey Castle and running westwards towards Beddingham and Lewes via Polegate and Selmeston. The present access road to The Green House appears to be a surviving segment of this road, along with its continuation eastwards, heading towards Arlington and Polegate. There nevertheless is a problem with identifying this old and fairly straight track as a Roman road, because when we look at the 1840 Tithe Map we can see no sign of the Slubby Lane link between the site of The Green House and Stonery Farm. The lane is shown running from the churchyard past the sandpit to The Green House as it does today, but from there, on the Tithe Map, it curves round towards the north. Perhaps the 'old way' between Green House and Stonery Farm, the Roman road, was revived after the time of the Tithe Map. It is possible, but there are clearly dangers in making too many assumptions from alignments gleaned from modern maps.

The Roman road turned sharply left, southwards, at Selmeston churchyard, to turn right at the junction with the modern A27 and from there follows the line of the A27 westwards. This is very interesting, in that it implies that the road running west from Pevensey, not exactly straight but nearly so, was heading for some kind of landmark at the Slubby Lane-

Street junction, in other words Selmeston churchyard. The church did not exist in the Romano-British period, but perhaps something else was standing on the churchyard site.

Ivan Margary gives a detailed map showing his reconstruction of the Roman road junction at Selmeston churchyard.[7] He shows the present lane running west from Stonery Farm as exactly following the line of the Roman road for part of the way, but as the lane approaches The Street it deviates from it. Margary's Roman road continues in a straight line to the church site, in other words it runs east-west right across the churchyard. In a similar way, the southern (straight) segment of The Street exactly follows the line of a southwest-northeast Roman road running out into the Weald. But whereas the modern road curves slightly to avoid the churchyard, Margary has the Roman road continuing in a straight line, again crossing the churchyard. The two Roman roads met at the church.

Margary does not ask, or explain, why the Roman road from Pevensey would aim so purposefully for the church, when the church itself would not have existed. Something must have existed on the site for the road to have aimed for it. If not, a simpler route could have been devised, taking the road from Berwick Common directly to the Barley Mow Corner, avoiding the unnecessary dog-leg south-westwards along The Street. Presumably Margary's thinking was that the Roman road junction would have become a focus that later attracted the building of a church and the establishment of a burial ground.

A careful reading of Margary's paper reveals that behind most of his Pevensey-Glynde road route there is a complete lack of evidence. There are certain places, such as Glynde and Polegate, where he is able to point to physical remains of a Roman road. But at Selmeston he offers no physical evidence whatever. Margary offers no archaeological or topographic evidence for Roman roads crossing the churchyard. It appears from the literature that there isn't any. It is quite possible that the road system in the Romano-British period was after all not drawn out with a ruler, but instead included bends and curves. In that case, there is no reason to suppose that the present line of The Street (not quite straight) and the present line of Slubby Lane (also not quite straight) do anything other than faithfully follow the route of the roads as they were nearly two thousand years ago. If we allow that the bends and curves and slight changes of direction are original features of the ancient road network, the churchyard, or rather the space that became the churchyard, may itself have been part of the Romano-British landscape.

A stone circle?

The circularity of the churchyard argues for its being ancient, certainly pre-Conquest, but how ancient? The fact that it seems to coincide with some sort of focus in the second, third and fourth centuries AD suggests that there was an ancient meeting place, perhaps a ceremonial centre, already established on the churchyard site.

On the south-east perimeter of the churchyard, and about nine metres in from its boundary ditch, a large sarsen stone lies prone on the ground, its flat and very smooth upper surface flush with the land surface.

This has all the characteristics of a natural sarsen, a dense close-grained sandstone, buff-brown in colour, and with a couple of irregular holes in it.

The holes in sarsen stones are thought to be fossil root-holes, dating back millions of years to the time when the rock was still a layer of loose sand. The smoothness of this slab, which measures 1.5m by 1.1m, may be natural or the result of deliberate dressing, like the inner faces of some of the huge sarsens at Stonehenge.

The sarsen stone may once have stood upright on its outer edge, which is very level, and subsequently fallen northwards towards the centre of the enclosure. Neolithic megalith builders sometimes seated their stones in deep sockets to ensure that they would stand for ever, yet sometimes perched them precariously

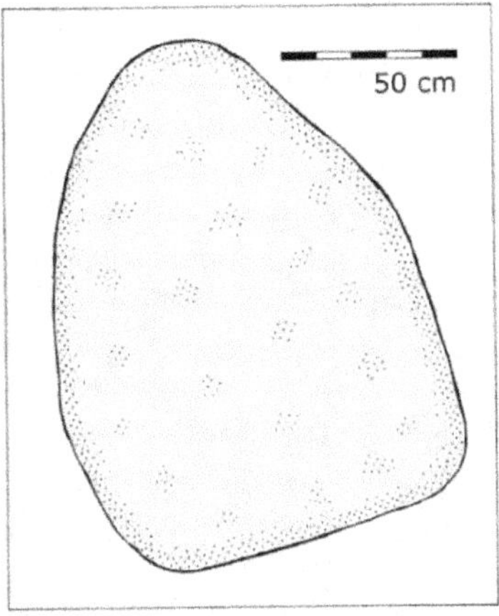

Plan of the sarsen stone

in shallow sockets, propping them up with packing stones. These badly built megaliths later fell over. Standards of workmanship were as variable then as they are today. Arbor Low in Derbyshire is a classic case of a stone circle that was poorly built. Every single stone at Arbor Low today lies flat on the ground. The collapse is so total that some archaeologists have even wondered if the stones were perhaps intended from the start to lie flat. So we could not be sure whether the Selmeston sarsen was raised on its broad flat end and later fell inwards or was raised more precariously on its pointed end and later fell outwards. A small-scale archaeological excavation might determine whether a pit exists under one end or the other, and also in itself provide evidence that this sarsen was once a standing megalith.

The combination of a circular enclosure and a single sarsen stone offers the tantalizing possibility that at Selmeston we have a previously unrecognized megalithic site, perhaps even a stone circle. We know from the finds in the nearby sandpit that people were living here in the Mesolithic and Neolithic, so it is not impossible that they created a ceremonial centre of some kind here. It would be exceptional, though. As far as I am aware, no other stone circle site is known in Kent, Surrey or Sussex.

Arbor Low stone circle, Derbyshire: a circle of fallen stones

For the moment, pending an archaeological investigation, the question must be left hanging in the air. There is a possibility that Selmeston churchyard is the site of a stone age ceremonial monument. If one or more stones were still standing when the Romans arrived, it would explain why, if Ivan Margary was right, the Roman road from Pevensey led purposefully westwards towards Selmeston churchyard. A standing monument would have been a conspicuous landmark, an obvious point in the landscape on which to align a road, especially as it stood on the low, dry Greensand ridge. It might at that time still have been a gathering-place for the local community.

Sarsen stones have always presented farmers with a problem, obstructing ploughing, and often naturally occurring boulders have, over many centuries, been moved to the field edge, to prevent obstruction. But this large boulder has not been moved to a field edge. It does not lie half-hidden in a hedgerow; it has been deliberately hauled to the churchyard enclosure and dragged another nine metres inside it. This does not look like typical field clearance.

Perhaps a megalithic monument stood on this site, but it takes more than one sarsen stone to prove that there was a stone circle here and no other sarsens are visible in the enclosure.

We move on in time now, leapfrogging the bronze age and iron age to return briefly to the period of the Roman occupation. Isolated Romano-British artefacts have been found throughout the area, showing that the area was occupied or at least visited during the Roman occupation. Some earthworks to the north of the village, but south of the railway line, on the east side of The Street are thought to be Romano-British.

~

~ 3 ~

Selmeston in the Dark Ages

The Saxons

The Saxon village of Selmeston was established early, between AD 400 and 600. A major early Saxon cemetery site lies on the west side of The Street opposite Church Farm, both behind and beneath Manor Cottages, about 200 metres north-north-east of the church.[1] This was among the earliest Saxon cemeteries in Sussex, one of half a dozen burial sites established by Saxon pioneers between the Ouse and the Cuckmere. And for each cemetery there must have been a settlement nearby.

In 1897 the first two Saxon graves were discovered by chance when the foundations were being dug for Manor Cottages. The grave goods included a gilt copper alloy saucer brooch, a glass cone beaker, a fragment of a glass bowl, pottery bowls and twenty-two beads, some made of amber. There was also iron weaponry, including a spearhead, an axehead, a knife, a shield boss and fragments of a sword.[2] These important artefacts were kept at Sherrington Manor until 1950, when they were given to the Sussex Archaeological Society.

In that year workmen were digging a trench in the Manor Cottage gardens under the direction of Mr H. A. Davis, a builder and archaeologist who lived at Selmeston. They found several weapons including an iron sword.

In 1963, a dozen more Saxon graves in the same area were excavated under the direction of Mr D. Thomson. The finds were not published. In 1979, Martin Welch of University College London (UCL) excavated the field to the west, behind the cottages, the large field known as Troy Town. Another fourteen graves were uncovered there in what was emerging as one of the largest Anglo-Saxon cemeteries in the south of England. It contains over 200 Saxon graves, dating from the fifth, sixth and seventh centuries AD.

Saxon Finds

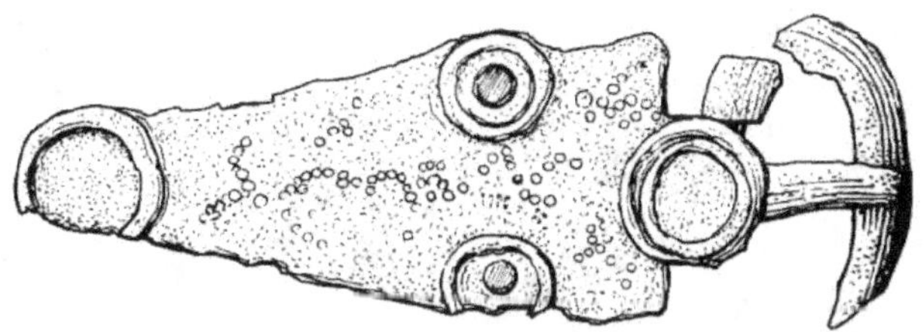

An Anglo-Saxon belt buckle

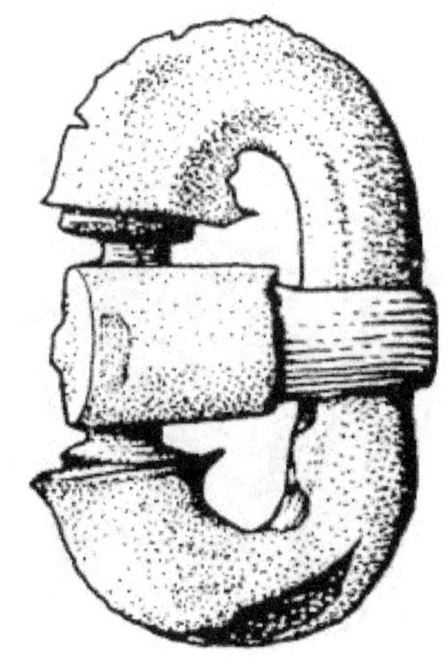

Another belt buckle

Beads from Selmeston Grave 16A

An Anglo-Saxon saucer brooch

Among other objects found in the cemetery was a wooden bucket with bronze fittings, with the wood still in good condition. This was found together with swords decorated in gilt, eighteen spears, twenty-six daggers, bronze and enamel brooches and pottery of an unusual design. A unique hexagonal shield boss was found.[3]

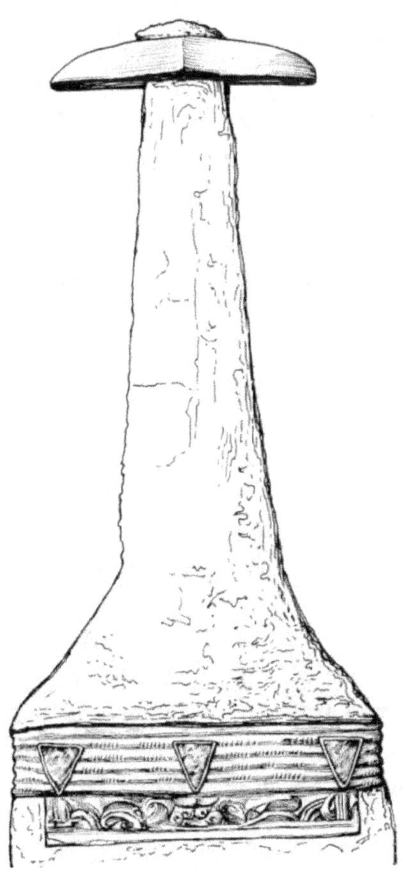

The handle of an Anglo-Saxon sword from Selmeston

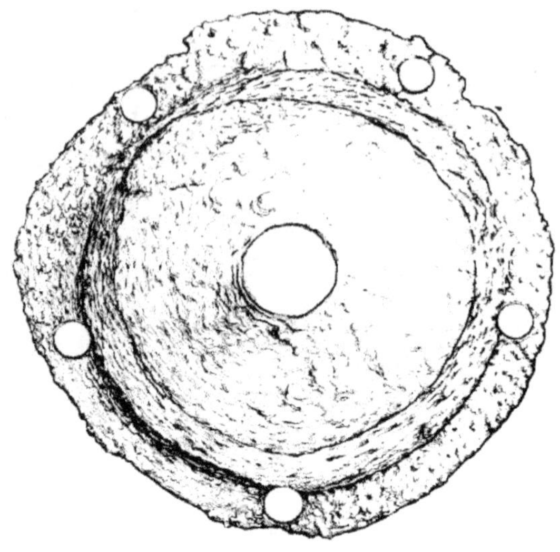

An Anglo-Saxon shield boss found at Selmeston

The finds from this major dig are stored at the Institute of Archaeology at UCL. It is regrettable that this hoard of Saxon finds is not on public display in Sussex, but at least some items have been released for display in Lewes. These include two necklaces, one of nine amber beads, the other a more colourful variety of glass beads. Some of the Selmeston finds, redrawn, are illustrated here.

In July 2015, a student from UCL, Scott Chausee, carried out a geophysical survey of the whole of Troy Town. The survey shows that there are probably many more graves beyond the area of the original dig. It is to be hoped that this will lead on in time to a more extensive excavation by the UCL team. One point that needs to be resolved is why all of the Selmeston graves seen so far seem to be the graves of men. The absence of women among the burials is marked. Were the women buried elsewhere? Perhaps elsewhere in the same large field?

Selmeston is one of the special group of very early Saxon burial sites in the Ouse-Cuckmere block. There were other early cemeteries at Sanctuary, on the low ridge between Berwick and Alfriston, and at Bishopstone. Selmeston has provided a key part of the critical evidence that this area of Sussex between the Ouse and the Cuckmere was the earliest in Sussex to have been colonized by Germanic settlers at the beginning of the fifth century AD. The undulating land surface in the vicinity of the Anglo-Saxon cemetery suggests that there was a settlement adjoining and it is likely that future archaeology in this area may yield further evidence of the Anglo-Saxon occupation.[4]

But this is by no means the end of Selmeston's Saxon story. There was another, separate, site not far away and it was, remarkably, the same sandpit that yielded the remains of the Neolithic and Mesolithic dwellings. The sandpit site, at TQ 515066, produced two clay loom weights that were of late Saxon type and late Saxon pottery fragments. Some horses' teeth were also found in the remains of a hearth.[5] This evidence points directly to habitation on the sandpit site, which is only 150 metres from the churchyard. This in turn suggests that the churchyard may have been a focus at that time, and there may already have been an early church standing on the churchyard site in the two centuries before the Norman Conquest.

~

~ 4 ~

Medieval and Early Modern Selmeston

The medieval parish

Place names are often a puzzle to local historians, and the derivations cooked up by Victorian scholars are equally often little more than guesses. Known early forms of the name Selmeston include easily recognizable close variations such as Selmseston and Silmestone (in the reign of Edward IIII), and Sielmestone in the Domesday Book. The pronunciation of the name has in the past been simplified to 'Simpson', although these days, with increased literacy, spelling pronunciation has spread far and wide and nearly everyone pronounces it '*sell*-mess-turn'. Spelling pronunciation has also given us the widespread use of 'Bishop-<u>stone</u>', when the Saxon origin of the name, *Bishop's tun*, the bishop's estate, clearly indicates that it should be pronounced '<u>Bish</u>ops-tern'. It has been suggested though not proved that 'Selmeston' derives from the Anglo-Saxon place name *Sigehelm's tun*. Sige helm means 'victory helmet', which may have been a man's name, and perhaps even the name of the leader of the early Saxon community that first settled here.[1]

The building we now see in the churchyard is certainly not the original church, but a replica of the medieval structure. That medieval building may in its turn have stood on the site of an even earlier building. It has been suggested that the footprint of the original late Saxon or early Norman church may survive in the floor-plan of current building.[2] If so, this is an interesting parallel to nearby Berwick church, where I found that the combined length of the nave and chancel was the same as the combined length of the nave and choir at Bishopstone, which is a known Saxon building. Selmeston church is the same length again, to within a few centimetres.

Selmeston church is the only church in the Rape of Pevensey to be mentioned in the Domesday survey, which gives us firm documentary evidence that Selmeston had a late Saxon church. Of the Sussex churches known to have existed in the middle of the eleventh century, the time of the Norman Conquest, all were fitted with chancels as well as naves, but none of them had towers. This well describes Selmeston church today; it still has no tower. Its design is therefore significantly closer to that of its Saxon predecessor than either Berwick or Bishopstone.

Selmeston in the Hundred of Wandelmestrie is mentioned twice in the 1086 Domesday Survey, where the two big houses in the parish, Sherrington Manor and Tilton House, are also mentioned. Sherrington was also known in medieval documents as Elerintone, Serintone and Sirintone; Tilton was alternatively known as Tilintone. Modern village houses haphazardly line the village street, as might be expected. Some of them probably stand on the sites of lost medieval houses, but there are also traces of unresurrected medieval houses in the fields flanking the street.

Some of the present houses date from the middle ages, such as Fairland, which stands beside the entrance to the old drive to Sherrington Manor, the drive that shows up as a slightly sunken green lane running straight across the field behind Fairland. Other houses have been recycled out of the materials from demolished medieval houses. From the seventeenth century onwards, village houses have been built of brick and flint. Many of the older houses have names reflecting their former use. Church Farm, built just to the north of the church in 1548, stands on the site of an earlier house that had stood on the same spot since at least as early as 1288. The Green House, built in about 1600, is another house with an earlier ancestry; it was originally a thirteenth century Wealden hall house, very likely built by a yeoman farmer. The Green House was also used as a priest's safe house at the time of the Reformation. Wheelwrights was built in about 1570. The Old Poor House was built in 1640 and East View in 1650.

The southern part of the parish, on the slightly higher and drier Greensand outcrop, may have been partially cleared of woodland early on, even as early as the Mesolithic, when the Greensand was a focus of activity. The fields in this area, the area south of the churchyard, are larger and more regular, reflecting early woodland clearance. The northern part, on the Weald Clay, remained wooded until much later. The later clearance is indicated by smaller and less regular fields. Many of the species-rich hedgerows are thought to be remnants of larger areas of woodland, so that they are in effect narrow strips of surviving ancient wildwood. The fields are often bounded by these 'shaws'. Even when land was needed for agriculture, it was still in everyone's interest to conserve strips of woodland to provide timber for house-building and fencing, and to provide firewood.

The Street itself is thought to have originated as a drove road. Drove roads were routes along which livestock were driven seasonally, from the milder winter pastures near the coast into the Vale of Sussex for summer grazing. The Street appears to have been used to connect the Wealden summer grazing via Bo-peep Lane, the Greenway, Firle Road and Blatchington Hill with coastal pastures at Seaford. In fact, once over the South Downs escarpment, the Greenway route split at the Blackstone into several branches, so that livestock might be taken to several (winter) destinations from Chyngton in the east to Bishopstone in the west.

Drove roads are traditionally thought of as being medieval, and they were certainly in use in the middle ages, but it is possible that they were in use much earlier, perhaps as early as the iron age.[3] Archaeologists excavating the Anglo-Saxon cemetery in Troy Town, immediately to the west of the Street and north of the Church, found evidence that an early road ran through it, possibly Romano-British but more likely iron age in origin. On the other hand this second potential drove road would have been only a few tens of metres west of The Street; it seems rather unlikely that two parallel drove roads would exist so close together.

The Street is marked out as an old road by its sunken nature, gradually worn down by cartwheels, especially in the north. Even as it passes the churchyard it is noticeably down at a lower level than either the churchyard or the Rectory's front lawn.

The village shrank during the fourteenth century, partly as a result of shifts in land use, partly as a result of the Black Death. The plague may also have been responsible for taking out the village of Sidenore, which is thought to have stood somewhere to the north of Selmeston village.

John Ellman of Glynde was responsible for developing the Southdown breed of sheep, and he was consulted continually on every subject by Lord Sheffield. As a result of these discussions, in 1786 Lord Sheffield set up a wool fair at Lewes. Bringing the flock-masters together in this way was a huge step forward in helping them to secure a proper price for their wool.

Perhaps prompted by the success of the Lewes wool fair, Lord Egremont set up an annual sheep fair near Petworth in West Sussex in 1795. Like Lord Sheffield, Lord Egremont consulted John Ellman. At about the same time, and almost certainly on Ellman's advice, a small annual sheep and cattle fair was set up at Selmeston. It was held every September on the Fair Field to the south of the village. By the end of the eighteenth century Selmeston Sheep Fair had become an important stock fair. Selmeston's position at the foot of the Downs made it a good meeting-place for Downland stock farmers living to the east of Lewes, Wealden farmers and graziers to the north, and dealers from London.[4]

John Ellman of Glynde

The mound of prizes offered at these fairs helped to encourage breeders to persevere harder in the improvement of their stock. John Ellman both instigated and provided the prizes. He was generous with advice too. As a result of all this activity, Ellman became a significant public figure, nationally and internationally. In 1798, the Emperor of Russia ordered two Southdown rams from Ellman, through George III. Ellman was unsure how to set a price for his rams, so he asked the Duke of Bedford to do it. The Duke set the price at 300 guineas, and ordered a pair of Ellman's rams for himself at the same price. The Duke was frequently a companion of the Prince of Wales at Brighton, but often absented himself to go over to Glynde to stay with Ellman. On one occasion, when he rejoined the Prince at Lewes Racecourse, the Prince asked him where he had been, and the Duke said, 'Please, your Royal Highness, I have been farming with my friend Ellman.' When in 1833 Thomas Ellman won the gold medal at the Smithfield Show for a Southdown sheep everyone acknowledged that Ellman's sheep were the best ever exhibited.[5]

~

In 1425, a hearing was called at Selmeston to determine the age of a villager by the name of William Selwyn. The date of William's birth had to be established to confirm that he had reached the age of 21 and was therefore old enough to inherit property. Three witnesses came forward to confirm that William was born on 24 August 1403. The first was William Gyle, who remembered the day of William Selwyn's baptism. He had been that day to see the hanging corpse of William Colley, who had committed suicide at Eastbourne. When he returned he met a woman who was carrying the infant William to be baptized. A second witness, Robert Proudfoot, said that his tenant John Yford was on the day of William Selwyn's birth seized and abducted by the French and taken to Harfleur. It is a surprise to discover that French raiders came this far inland; the implication is that they had come northwards through Seaford and Blatchington, via the Greenway, Bo-peep and Alciston, along the drove road. Another witness, John Hendyman, remembered the day because immediately after William Selwyn's baptism he had broken his leg while playing football. In 1403 and 1404, games of football were regularly played as part of the baptism ceremony. Football was a violent game, resulting in injuries. By 1410, the authorities were imposing fines for allowing this dangerous and antisocial game to be played.

The Selwyn case is a reminder that medieval Sussex was a very different place from today's Sussex. Today there is no escape from the law, but in the middle ages it was possible for law-breakers to take refuge in churches. Of all the churches in the area in 1287, for some reason Selmeston was the only one to which fugitives fled for sanctuary.

Troy Town

As we saw earlier, a Saxon cemetery was discovered in the field separating Sherrington Manor from the Street. This field is named on the Tithe Map (surveyed by William Figg in 1840) as Troy Town.

The name is significant as it was the name commonly given in the middle ages to turf mazes. Three Troy Town mazes survive, at St Agnes on the Isles of Scilly, Somerton near Banbury in Oxfordshire and on the roadside near Dalby in North Yorkshire. This last maze is known as The City of Troy. Only three Troy Towns survive. At least six more have been lost: there was one near Dorchester and another on a hill between Farnham and Guildford. There was a maze called 'The Walls of Troy' with an odd dodecagonal design between Marfleet and Paull on Holderness. Another 'Walls of Troy' existed between Brough and Rockliffe in Cumbria. Troy-town at Pimperne in Dorset was destroyed in 1730; it had an unusual design consisting of random wandering paths.

The field name Troy Town at Selmeston is significant, carrying with it the intriguing possibility that the village once had its own turf maze. As far as I know, there is no tradition or folk memory of it. The field in question was the site of the Anglo-Saxon cemetery, but perhaps by the middle ages the location of the unmarked graves had been forgotten and the field was simply re-used. But even if the cemetery was remembered and respected, Troy Town is a very large field, and there would have been room enough in it for a cemetery and a maze. Usually turf mazes were relatively small - the Mizmaze in Dorset was about thirty metres across – while Troy Town field is 250 metres long.

The name Troy Town was at one time assumed to be a reference to the legendary labyrinthine layout of the city of Troy in Homer, but a case has been made for a different origin. William Stukeley noted that the mazes in Wales were known by the name of 'Caertroi'. 'Caer' means town in Brittonic, the ancient British language, and 'troi' means 'winding' or 'turning'.

The handful of turf mazes that still exist today have only survived because they have been carefully maintained, usually by the local community. One of the best preserved is the Dalby turf maze, the City of Troy.

The beautifully preserved City of Troy at Dalby in North Yorkshire

Unless they are regularly trimmed and recut, the ditches of turf mazes grass over and begin to fill with soil. In time, the design becomes very indistinct and eventually disappears. This is what has happened to the Mizmaze at Leigh in Dorset. It is under pasture and can be visited, but at ground level its shape is very indistinct because it has been grassed over for a long time. A low bank can be made out, enclosing a hexagonal space, and there is a low rise at the centre, but the design of the probably circular maze itself, within the octagon, has been lost.

The overall shape of the Mizmaze can best be seen from the air, but it is evident that this probably medieval maze is close to extinction. It is only the enclosing bank that allows us to identify its site at all. So the absence of any sign of a Selmeston Troy

The Mizmaze in Dorset

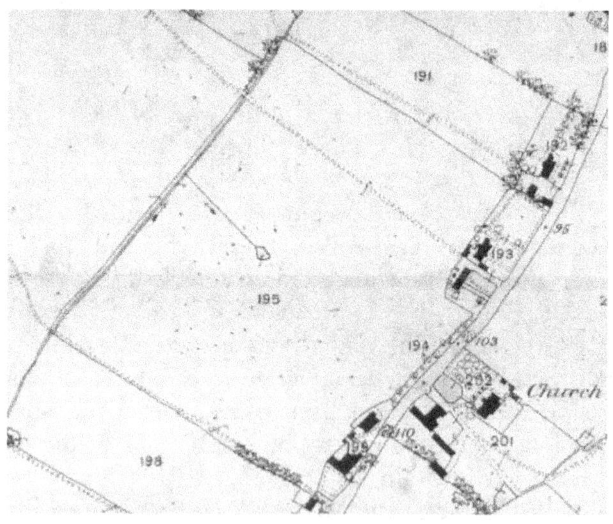

Troy Town at Selmeston
Note the incorrectly identified church; maps can't always be trusted.

Town tells us that it may have passed on to the next stage - extinction. It has completely vanished into the evolving turf. It is unlikely that it is hidden beneath the prominent central clump of trees, because that is the site of a spring-fed pond.

On the right of the satellite photo is the northern segment of the Street, and Sherrington Manor is just off the picture to the left. Towards the top of the photo, it is just possible to make out the faint line of the original straight entrance drive connecting Sherrington Manor to the Street.

Tudor Selmeston

The fine tomb in the chancel commemorating Lady Beatrice Bray (J04) was probably built at the orders of her husband, Sir Edward Bray. He was born in or before 1492, the year of Columbus's landmark first voyage to the New World. Like Columbus, Sir Edward Bray was a sea-captain. While Columbus skippered the *Santa Maria*, Sir Edward Bray was captain of the ill-fated *Mary Rose*, Thomas Howard's flagship, in 1513, and then captain of the *Magdaleyn of Founteraby* in 1514.

The Mary Rose

Bray held several manors in Surrey and Sussex, and was responsible for musters in Surrey in 1531. He was sheriff of Surrey and Sussex in 1538-9, high treasurer for the army against the French in 1545 and in 1556-57 constable of the Tower of London. His specific connection with Selmeston stems from the acquisition of one of the Selmeston manors, which he purchased from John Gage in 1532. There were three manors in the parish, Ludlay, Tilton and Sherrington. It was Sherrington manor that Sir Edward Bray acquired.

Sir Edward had three wives. The first was Elizabeth Lovell, the second Beatrice Shirley, and the third Jane Browne. It was Beatrice, the second wife, who was buried in Selmeston church in 1532. She was born in 1480, the daughter of Ralph Shirley of Staunton Harold. Her first husband was Edward Elrington (or Elderton) of London; Sir Edward Bray was her second husband. She was the mother of Edward Elrington MP, Richard Elrington of Preston, Sir Edward Bray of Shere, Owen Bray and Beatrix Bray. She died in 1532 and was buried in the chancel at Selmeston.

Sir Edward himself asked to be buried in Cranleigh church, in 1558.

In the manor rolls there is a mention of Thomas Gyles, a bondman living at Selmeston: 'Thomas his son lives with Edward Bray knight'.[8] Presumably Thomas Gyles junior worked as a servant in Sir Edward's household, either at Sherrington Manor or in Surrey.

In 1533, the year after the death of Beatrice Bray, Sir Edward disposed of some land in Selmeston. Sir Edward and feoffees, Sir Richard Sherley, Richard Andrewes, Thomas Sherley and Edward Elderton granted a freehold tenement to John Thetcher of Selmeston. It consisted of the following:
1) The Oldeland, an eleven acre piece of land along the side of Hony Lane,

2) A six acre piece of land separated from the common field of Sherrington and alongside John Thetcher's land called South Horam,

3) The Krinkk, a one and a half acre piece of land beside the common field of Sherrington.[9.]

~

The Selmeston parish register was begun in 1563, a long delayed response to the command that baptisms, weddings and burials were to be recorded. The first volume of the present register has, inside its front cover, a note that 'The Old Register which began in the year 1563 and continued to the present year 1667 is to be found in the Church Chest.' Unfortunately it is not there any longer. This early volume was lost some time after 1780, which is when Sir William Burrell read it and copied extracts from it for his Sussex Collections (now at the British Library).

A new bell was hung in the belfry in the year of Elizabeth I's death, inscribed 'Joseph Hatch made me 1603'.

In the seventeenth century the value of the land at Selmeston was surprisingly high. In 1649, the 1,590 acres of the parish of Selmeston was valued at £748, compared with East Dean (£403), Berwick (422), Alciston (£435) and Bishopstone (£459).[10]

Sherrington Manor

The parish of Selmeston is shared among three manors. Each is represented by a manor house, with Tilton in the south and Ludlay in the north. Sherrington in the centre, not far from the church, was a major moated manor house in the middle ages. A view of the site drawn by Grimm in 1787 shows some impressive remains flanking the central brick-built range, which is what survives today.

In the mid-fourteenth century John Selwyn married Katherine, the heiress of Simon Sherrington, and the Selwyn family remained at Sherrington until the early sixteenth century. Then Thomas Selwyn decided to move to the estate at Friston which his wife had inherited from her grandfather.

In 1626 Matthias Caldicott purchased Sherrington. Caldicott was a man of obscure origins who became a servant of Richard Sackville, third Earl of Dorset. He worked in the earl's households at Dorset House in London and Knole in Kent. Caldicott became a friend and favourite of the earl, who familiarly called him Matti, and he was a witness to the earl's clandestine marriage to the great heiress Lady Anne Clifford. But Caldicott was by no means a favourite of the new bride, who complained of his 'ill offices' and tried to block the advantageous marriage the earl was arranging for him. Where the blame lay is impossible to tell, because the relationship between Lady Anne and the earl was also a turbulent one. She had a powerful personality and there was a great deal of friction between her and her husband. The earl was extravagant, as well as frequently unfaithful. He has been described as 'one of the seventeenth century's most accomplished gamblers and wastrels.' Among his mistresses were Venetia Stanley and Lady Penistone, who was the wife of Sir Thomas Penistone, a member of the earl's retinue.

Matthias Caldicott was present at the earl's deathbed in March 1624. He was not a beneficiary of the earl's will, not because he had fallen out of favour, but because the earl had provided for him already with generous gifts. By 1626 Matthias Caldicott was rich enough to be able to buy Sherrington manor.

Caldicott himself died in 1647 leaving his son a diamond ring given to him by the Earl of Dorset; he left his son-in-law a chest of viols embellished with 'the arms of my late noble and much honoured lord.'

The Matthias Caldicott who was buried at Selmeston (in plot J09) in 1719 aged 65 was probably a grandson of the earl's favourite. The Caldicott family declined socially through the succeeding generations until they ranked only as farmers. To give an indication of this descent, in 1800 Matthias Caldicott of

Richard Sackville, 3rd Earl of Dorset,
accomplished gambler and wastrel

Sherrington (1755-1808) was fined for evading the Lewes Market tolls by buying chickens illicitly. This is the Matthias Caldicott who on his burial monument inside the church (J02) continues even today to boast, in large letters, that he was a GENTLEMAN – it was a vain boast. The same Matthias Caldicott ignored his brothers' children when drawing up his will, leaving Sherrington to Mary Hawes. She married an

Alfriston doctor, James Skinner, in 1811. Mary Skinner died in 1819 (J10) and by the time of the 1831 census James Skinner was farming Sherrington. He died in 1873 and his daughter Mary inherited the manor (J06). She was the wife of Richard Billiter of the Barcombe oil-mills.

Only the central range of Sherrington Manor survived the extensive rebuilding of 1874.[13]

~

~ 5 ~

Modern Selmeston

Stanton Collins

The old church at Selmeston is said to have had an altar tomb, a tomb in the graveyard that was built right up against the east wall of the chancel. It was adjacent to the altar inside the church, hence its name, perhaps, but with a loose lid. According to tradition, this tomb was used as a temporary store for contraband by the Alfriston Gang led by Stanton Collins. Also according to tradition, a barrel of smuggled cognac was occasionally left by the Alfriston Gang at the vicarage door, as a kind of rough rental for the use of the altar tomb.

The stories that circulated about the Alfriston Gang were the inspiration for Rudyard Kipling's poem *A Smuggler's Song*.

If you wake at midnight, and hear a horse's feet,
Don't go drawing back the blind, or looking in the street,
Them that asks no questions they isn't told a lie.
Watch the wall, my darling, when the Gentlemen go by! [1]

Several slightly different versions of Stanton Collins' life of crime are in circulation, and because they have become the stuff of folklore it is difficult to separate true history from romance. He is said to have used the Market Cross Inn at Alfriston as his headquarters. It is because of this story that the pub is now called The Smugglers Inn. In Stanton Collins's day, the first three decades of the nineteenth century, it was known as the Market Cross House or Inn.

The building, dating from the fourteenth century, seems to have been designed to enable smugglers to hide or escape if there was a raid by customs officers. It was a rabbit warren of a place, with 21 rooms, 47 doors and six staircases. There were secret hiding places in the cellars and the attics. There is no record of customs officials ever raiding Alfriston successfully. The Stanton Gang as Collins's company of smugglers was known was efficient and effective, and it seems they were never caught. It must have helped them that the entire village was involved actively or passively in smuggling.

The story of the Stanton Gang has often been repeated as part of Alfriston's persona as a tourist honeypot. But how much truth is there in it? Did Stanton Collins really exist? If so, was he a criminal? Was he a smuggler? There is in fact positive historical proof that he existed and that he was involved in crime. As things turned out, he was caught not for smuggling but for another crime. The South Downs National Park website tells us that he was convicted for sheep-stealing, but that seems not to be true. A piece in the *Independent* mentioned that he was convicted of barn-burning, but that is questionable too.

There is a Home Office document with the title 'Criminal Petitions', dating from January 1835. It relates to a petition organized by the family of Stanton Collins, and signed by 56 other people, asking for clemency for him. It refers to his conviction at the Sussex Winter Assize at Lewes four years earlier, on 12 December 1831 – for stealing barley. Specifically, Stanton Collins stole barley from Thomas Jenner of Litlington, and he was sentenced to seven years' transportation for this offence – a severe sentence by the standards of the time if this was a first offence, which of course it may not have been. Collins was probably held on a prison hulk on the Thames or Medway estuary until he was shipped to Australia, aboard the *Lord William Bentinck* in April 1832, along with 185 other convicts. He was delivered to Van Diemen's Land on 28 August 1832.[2]

The rather late petition to commute his sentence was instigated by a group of petitioners: the MP J. R. Kemp, James and Mary Collins, Stanton's parents, John, Caleb and Mark Collins, Stanton's brothers, Elizabeth Waters and Catherine Collins, his sisters, and John Waters, his brother-in-law. Their grounds for clemency were that Stanton was previously of good character and that his conduct both in prison and after transportation to Australia had been good. The family argued that before he committed the offence he had started drinking and had been keeping bad company. In fact the Gaoler's report described his character as 'bad', though the family were able to produce a certificate of good behaviour from Thomas Ancell, the keeper of the House of Correction in Lewes and it was alleged that his master where he was working in Hobart Town placed great trust in him. On the other hand there was a letter from Mr Gage arguing against mitigation of sentence because Stanton Collins was a known member of a gang of smugglers. He had form.

It seems that Mr Gage's intervention swung the case firmly against Collins, and the outcome of the petition is crisply and succinctly recorded as - 'Nil'.

With Stanton Collins's removal from the scene, the Alfriston smuggling operation seems to have faded away. Without Stanton there was no Stanton Gang.

As for Stanton Collins's association with the Market Cross House, some new information has unexpectedly come to light. Collins is said in some accounts to have used the inn as his headquarters, and other sources say that he owned the house. A TV programme spawned by the hugely successful *Time Team* series, *Pub Dig*, featured The Smugglers at Alfriston. Some excavation in the back garden uncovered clear evidence that a slaughter-house had stood there in the nineteenth century. In the Home Office Criminal Petitions record, Stanton Collins is noted to be 35 years old — and a *'butcher* from Alfriston'. So his connection with the building is corroborated.

In the popular imagination, smuggling was a fun activity, mainly enjoyable because it involved outwitting the authorities, and a lot of covert nocturnal activity, but the Stanton Gang was notorious for its callousness, ruthlessness and cruelty. On one occasion, the gang was hiding among the gorse on the cliffs overlooking Cuckmere Haven, waiting for a signal from the boats that their cargo had been landed. The signal came and they were about to make their way down to the beach when a Revenue Officer appeared on the cliff top. As was usual at night, he was finding his way by following the line of chalk blocks that marked the path. But the smugglers had anticipated this and moved the rocks so that they led the Revenue Officer over the cliff. With a cry, he fell, but just managed to throw out an arm and hang on to the edge. The gang rushed over to him from their hiding place. He begged them to save him, but they stamped on his hand and he fell to his death. The fall was believed to be an accident until long afterwards, when a deathbed confession by one of the smugglers revealed the truth.

The members of the Stanton or Alfriston Gang were involved in all kinds of criminal activity as well as smuggling. One of the gang members, Samuel Thorncraft, was eventually hanged for arson. The last surviving member was Bob Hall, who died in Eastbourne Workhouse in 1895 at the age of 94.

The Stanton Gang was dispersed by 1835, which means that any use of an altar tomb in the churchyard at Selmeston must also have ceased by 1835. The tomb that appears to occupy that position now (D01) is the grave of Maria Latham, the wife of one of Selmeston's vicars, the Revd Henry Latham. She died in 1846 so the grave must have been built at that time; it could not have existed in the time of Stanton Collins.

Henry Latham was the son of a London doctor, John Latham, and he matriculated at Brasenose College, Oxford in 1812 at the age of 17. In 1841 he was living at Selmeston with his wife Maria, who was then 45, and their two daughters, Diana (aged 15) and Elizabeth (8). Maria died in 1846 at the age of 50 and was buried in the churchyard on 8 September. Henry left Selmeston shortly after her death to make a fresh start as the vicar of Fittleworth. He married his second wife, Charlotte Roberts of Ashington, in 1848. In 1851 he was living in Fittleworth with Charlotte (aged 49), his unmarried daughter Diana (25) and stepdaughter Margaret (18). Henry Latham died in September 1866.[3]

The inscription on Maria Latham's grave is long and informative. It explains that Mrs Latham had a particular interest in seeing the children of the parish properly educated, to give them the best chance for the future, and that building a village school was a fitting tribute to her memory. The land where the school was to be built was given by the owner of Sherrington Manor, Dr James Skinner. Mary's husband, the Revd Henry Latham, provided most of the money for the building and work began at once. Initially there was just one classroom and accommodation for the schoolteacher. By 1866 there were 47 pupils. By 1873 there were 63; Latham's successor, the Revd Parish, had introduced a scheme to ensure regular attendance. By 1968, there were only 32 children attending the school, which was seen as no longer viable. The school is still there, but is now a private dwelling, The Flint House.

So, given that the structure we now see built up against the east wall of the chancel, the grave of Maria Latham (listed as D01 in the Monumental Inscriptions section of the book), was built in 1846, it cannot be connected with the story relating to the Stanton Gang and its smuggling activities, which had ceased over ten years earlier. It is also hard to believe that Henry Latham would have chosen to bury his wife at a spot that was associated with such nefarious activity, nor is it likely that a man of the cloth with substantial means would have re-used someone else's grave. The only conclusion that can be drawn from this is that the story associating the admittedly unusually located grave with the gang of smugglers was developed after Mrs Latham's death. Why? Presumably to account for the odd position of the grave, which almost looks as if it might have been designed to give discreet access to a vault beneath the chancel.

Was there anything at the east end of the chancel before 1846 and the building of Mary Latham's tomb? Two watercolour paintings date from the early nineteenth century: the George de Paris painting and the painting by Diana Latham. Diana Latham was the daughter of Maria and Henry Latham, who was the incumbent at Selmeston from 1833 to 1847. Both paintings show a high iron railing stretching right across between the two buttresses, apparently slightly bowed out into the churchyard. It is not clear what this railing was for, but it was probably added to enclose the Latham tomb and accentuate its status. It does not support the idea of an altar tomb. The fact that the 1803 Sharpe Collection painting shows neither railing nor tomb at the east end of the church supports the idea that both structures date from 1846. It also shows that the Latham tomb had no predecessor.

But the story does not end there. An anonymous article written for a journal in the 1880s and using information supplied by William Parish points to a different location, to the *south* of the chancel. This was described as 'an altar-tomb', in other words a tomb shaped like an altar, which is what might be termed a box, chest or table tomb. The pre-1866 photograph shows that there was indeed a chest tomb in the corner where the vestry now stands, though it was located well away from the chancel's south wall. 'The lid of this was loose and could be slid off without much difficulty. Village tradition explained as the reason for this that the tomb had been used as a receptacle for contraband merchandise in the old days when, it is feared, smuggling formed the staple occupation of a large proportion of the inhabitants of Sussex.'[4] This story is not much more credible than the other, though at least the tomb in question existed in the early decades of the nineteenth century; it was evidently demolished in 1866 to make room for the vestry.

Before leaving the Stanton Collins story, I have one final

The east end of the chancel in George de Paris's painting.

The east end of the chancel in Diana Latham's painting.

The east end of the church in 1803, with no railing and no tomb.
Note the asymmetrical buttresses.

reflection about the family's petition. The Collins family showed considerable audacity in presenting their petition, given that Stanton had already been transported and it must in any case have been widely known in Sussex that Stanton was involved in criminal activity and had been extremely lucky not to have been apprehended for smuggling.

Many people in the area must have known that he was actively involved in smuggling, and the Collins family might have expected that someone would come forward to say so – as Mr Gage did. If Stanton Collins had been at large, and in Sussex, it might not have been safe to denounce him. Smugglers could be savagely vengeful against those they believed had betrayed them.

Nineteenth century 'improvements'

In 1759 the new turnpike road (now the A27) was built, linking Lewes and Eastbourne. Before 1819, Common Lane was part of the main road to Eastbourne. It left the Old Coach Road at Bopeep Lane, then swung south of the site of Arlington Reservoir and on to the east to Swines Hill (now Polegate).

But now to Selmeston Church. Its vicar during the second half of the nineteenth century was William Parish who, as already mentioned, was a friend of Edward Ellman. Ellman had heavily restored his church at Berwick - some say over-restored - and this must have encouraged Parish to undertake a similar programme of radical improvements to his own medieval church a few years afterwards.[5] Alciston church nearby had also been restored in 1853.

The medieval church

Although the present church at Selmeston looks very like a medieval church, it was built in the middle of the nineteenth century, exactly on the footprint of the medieval building. The economist Maynard Keynes, who lived at Tilton in the south of the parish, discovered a watercolour painting in a London Art Shop and presented it to the church. The painting is a careful piece of work, showing a lot of architectural detail. It also has a handwritten caption, 'Selmeston Church, Sussex. Before alteration.' The painting is by George de Paris (1829-1911), who specialized in depicting Sussex churches.[6]

The painting clearly shows that in broad outline the medieval church was the same as the present-day church, though there are some differences in detail. Like the modern church, the medieval church had a south aisle but its south wall was supported by four north-south buttresses instead of three. A fifth buttress, oriented west-east, supported the south aisle's south-east corner, and close to it on the same alignment was a large chest tomb, mentioned in the last chapter. Today there is a vestry built into the south-east corner of the building, whereas in the medieval building there was an empty space. Significantly, there were two tall round-headed windows opening from this space to light the eastern end of the south aisle, and two tall square-headed windows in the south wall of the chancel, as well as what appears in the painting to be a high round-headed window. These extra windows would have let a significant amount of additional light into what is today a rather dark church. Filling this empty space with a vestry not only blocked all the windows but necessitated the removal of the chest tomb.

The Sharpe Collection painting of Selmeston church, also showing the view from the south-east, illustrates the same features, but in a little more detail. The two square-headed windows in the south wall of the chancel are subdivided by a transom about two-thirds of the way up, so that it is really a large rectangular window divided into four by a stone cross. The smaller round-headed window is shown not to be a window at all but a stone mural monument, placed surprisingly high up the wall.

The George de Paris painting shows the north-east and south-east corners of the chancel supported by two identical west-east oriented buttresses, each with two chamfers, one at the top and the other two-thirds of the way up. The 1803 Sharpe painting shows two distinctly different buttresses. The south-east buttress has chamfers at the top and halfway down, with a minor step near the bottom. The north-east buttress has a regular series of three chamfers in the upper half and a minor step near the bottom. The northern buttress is also noticeably thicker than the southern. These differences between the paintings may reflect a rebuilding of the southern buttress between 1803 and the 1840s.

There was a fire at Selmeston church in 1860. By 1867 the church was in such a poor state of repair that, Parish himself reputedly said, four sailors were able to pull it down in a day.[7] This suggests that the church was derelict and disintegrating, but there is a surviving watercolour (see below) showing the church shortly before its demolition, the George de Paris painting, and there is no sign in the picture of dereliction or imminent collapse. A pre-restoration photograph also shows the building apparently in good repair. If the building was in a dangerous state, one would have expected to see cracks in the walls and sagging roofs with missing tiles. The artist and the photographer show the church in what appears to be good condition. Whatever the truth of the situation, the church was demolished, right down to the ground, then immediately rebuilt in medieval style to look very much as it had before, but with a vestry added. Some of the floor was evidently left in place. One of the memorial slabs set in the nave floor (J01) has the northern chancel arch pier slightly overlapping one edge, which shows that the floor in that area was there before the Victorian wall. This stone was the memorial to Mary Allwork, who died in 1831. The stone slab is cracked parallel to the wall, and it is likely that the crack was caused by the weight of this new mid-nineteenth century wall, which was presumably built rather wider than its predecessor. Other memorial slabs set in the floor were moved to the vestry, as at Berwick.

The timbers of the old church were numbered so that as many of them as possible could be reused in the new building. The stones too were carefully re-used. The architect, Ewan Christian, rebuilt Selmeston church in typical fourteenth century Sussex style with flint walls, a roof of red clay tiles and a bell turret. The bell turret consisted of a low cube-shaped wooden belfry topped by a broach spire. This copied the design of the pre-1866 turret, except that the new spire was shorter. The old belfry appears to have been wooden, perhaps with horizontal louvres, like a beehive; now it is tile-hung.

The account of the church in Pevsner cannot be right in respect of the south aisle. The church is indeed built of flint and consists of a nave with a bell-turret and a chancel. But Pevsner goes on to say that 'the south aisle dates from the restoration of 1867 (E. Christian).' This cannot be right because the three-bay arcade supported on oak piers existed prior to the 1867 rebuild. Pevsner admits that the arcade pillars are 'apparently replacements of the original (fourteenth century) ones', so they must have existed to connect a fourteenth century south aisle to

Selmeston Church from the south-east, before demolition:
the George de Paris painting

the nave. The south aisle as we now see it may have been built by Ewan Christian, but to replace a pre-existing south aisle.

In the early nineteenth century, some believed the wooden columns were very old, perhaps even part of a pre-Norman church. This is unlikely. The oak columns are likely to date from the late fifteenth or early sixteenth century. The window at the east end of the south aisle was Late Perpendicular in style, and it is likely that the window, the pillars and the south aisle as a whole date from the end of the fifteenth century, not earlier.

When the time came to rebuild, it was found that the columns were rotten. They had to be replaced with new oak pillars.[8]

How different the original south aisle was from the present one is hard to tell, but it was certainly to some extent different. Both the pre-restoration de Paris painting (above) and a water-

An 1866 painting showing what the wooden pillars looked like just before the rebuilding. The nave is in the foreground, the south aisle beyond the pillars.

colour painting dating from 1803 show the exterior with *four* buttresses, when today there are three.

Arthur Mee, writing in 1937, described the wooden pillars 'that have stood here since the fourteenth century'; he overlooked the fact that what he saw were replacements. But he is certainly right to draw attention to the wooden pillars; they are rare.

Two pre-restoration watercolour paintings and a photograph show the original wooden pillars and the curved timber braces above them.[9]

Pevsner describes the oak pillars as octagonal (in section) and instead of arches they carry curved braces. In the chancel there is what Pevsner describes as a Late Perpendicular Easter Sepulchre, but it is (or perhaps was converted into) the tomb of Lady

Beatrice Bray. The stained glass in the chancel is by Charles Kempe, and dates from 1905.

The top of the altar consists of a stone six feet long and perhaps, as Arthur Mee tells us, cut many centuries ago. It may well predate the Parish rebuilding. So too may the delightful small carved wall bracket mounted on the south wall of the chancel. It depicts two stone winged angels among lilies, grapes and ears of wheat.

One of the features that came as standard with nineteenth century church improvement was a tiled floor. Selmeston, like Berwick, had to have its tiled floor. But with that came an attractive innovation, the many small diamond-shaped brass memorial tablets set amongst the floor tiles all along the central axis of the nave and chancel. These have kept their inscriptions well, still clear and perfectly legible after over a hundred years of being trodden under foot - and glittering in what is otherwise a rather gloomy church.

The complete rebuild presented the architect with a unique opportunity to introduce more light into the church. Ewan Christian (1814-1895) was an experienced architect, yet he did not seize this opportunity. He did add a window in the nave's west wall, but a larger west window with a lower sill would have been more effective. Then again, Christian was responsible for designing the south porches at St Peter's, East Blatchington, and St Leonard's, Seaford, and both of these structures are dark and heavy. Perhaps darkness is what Christian liked.

Ewan Christian was a worthy, plodding Victorian Gothicist; it is significant that other restoration projects he worked on have been condemned in outspoken terms.[10]

In the late nineteenth century, the newly rebuilt church was described as neat and well cared for as were the new parish schools.

The vicarage, inhabited by the Revd William Douglas Parish, was described as 'pleasantly situated'. Nearby Sherrington Place

Ewan Christian

was 'a fine old house standing among extensive pastures of good grazing land'. In 1886 there were 188 people living in the parish.[11] 'Selmeston, where there is a neat and well cared for church and parish schools. The vicarage, which is worth £208 per annum, with a pleasantly situated house, is held by the Rev William Douglas Parish, SCL, Trinity College, Oxford. One bell ('Joseph Hatch made me 1603'). There are 1,590 acres in this parish.'

Good Friday was celebrated in church but it was also a public holiday. In 1879, the vicar, William Parish, observed that his parishioners played marbles on Good Friday until the service was due to begin, continuing their games at the church gate until the last possible moment. As soon as the service was over they hurried out of church to resume their play, which went on for the rest of the day.[12]

Nineteenth century paintings of the church

Several nineteenth century watercolours of the church survive, and they show us what the building looked like before it was restored.[13]

Three of these have been mentioned already. One is the painting by George de Paris (below) which was found in a London art shop by Maynard Keynes, and probably painted between 1850 (when de Paris was 21) and 1860, certainly before 1866. Another is the 1803 painting from the Sharpe Collection (on the following page).

The George de Paris painting of Selmeston Church.

Like the de Paris painting, this picture shows the view of the church from the south-east. A significant difference between the two is that the 1803 painting shows asymmetrical buttresses attached to the east wall of the chancel. By the 1850s (see the picture above) the asymmetry had apparently been rectified. The northern buttress had been remade to match the southern.

The 1803 painting of Selmeston Church. View from the south-east.

The third picture (below) is the watercolour painting by Diana Latham, the vicar's daughter. The church is viewed from the NE.

The Latham and Sharpe pictures correctly show the church standing on a low knoll. The otherwise accurate de Paris painting does not really show this feature of the site.

Immediately before the medieval church was taken down and rebuilt in 1866-67, in February 1866 a set of watercolours was painted by an anonymous amateur artist.

They are unsigned, but clearly labelled. The intention was clearly to record the appearance of the church interior before the restoration began, either for posterity or as a guide to help the architect in his attempt to re-create the medieval building from the ground up.

These paintings are useful, but they are not totally reliable, as the sometimes faulty perspective indicates. One of the paintings (below) shows a diagonal view down the nave from the north-west towards the altar and the southern end of the south aisle, and is labelled 'Selmeston, Sussex, Feby 1866'.

The nave in February 1866.

A man standing on the left has just entered the church through the north door. On the right there are two wooden columns separating the nave from the south aisle, with wooden capitals and diagonal braces at the top. The braces on the north side support beams crossing the nave. Above this arcade the nave roof is shown rising vertically 6 or 8 feet to the top of the picture, which is hardly credible. East of the north porch there are wooden (box?) pews on both sides of the nave, but behind these there is what appears to be movable folding wooden seating.[14] Above the Early English chancel arch is a square panel bearing the royal coat of arms and the initials 'GR'. The nave floor is paved with rectangular stone slabs down each side, with what appears to be a brick-paved central aisle.

A second painting of the same view and evidently painted by the same artist is labelled 'Selmeston, Sussex 22nd February 1866.' It shows the braces attached to the wooden columns

A second view eastwards, up the nave, also painted in February 1866

differently. The braces run east and west, supporting what would have been the wall-brace. There are no braces going northwards to support the nave roof, nor are there any horizontal beams crossing the nave. But this painting shows the nave roof sloping up at 45 degrees as it should.

The square painting of the royal coat of arms with 'GR' is in place above the apex of the chancel arch. The nave floor has a central lane made of orange-red bricks, flanked on each side by three lines of rectangular stone slabs.[15]

The wooden columns and braces today.

A third painting shows the view from the Beatrice Bray tomb looking west-southwest towards the west end of the nave and the west end of the south aisle.

Like the first picture, this shows the two wooden columns capped by wooden capitals supporting diagonal braces which in turn support horizontal beams crossing the nave.

The box pews are shown continuing into the south side of the chancel. We might expect to be looking directly at the nave's west window, but oddly there is no west window- and no west door either. The painting's label is 'Selmeston Old Church, Sussex, 1866'.

This watercolour is corroborated by a retouched photograph (p 66) of the same view taken at about the same time. It shows the columns, beams and braces in the same way. It also shows the roof timbers of the south aisle spaced rather far apart as in the painting; today the roof timbers are closer together.

The view west, down the aisle, in February 1866.

The curving braces springing from the wooden columns.

A fourth painting shows the view northwards across the chancel towards the Bray tomb, and is labelled 'The Tomb of Beatrice Bray, 1532, Selmeston, Sussex, 22 Feb. 1866'. This was painted on the same day as the second painting. It shows the stone paved floor and three stone steps up to the plain wooden fence of the altar rail. The general design of the Bray tomb is recognizable, though the proportions are poorly represented. The northern part of the chancel arch and the front pews on the north side of the nave are shown.

The altar appears to be a stone tomb-like structure, with an arcaded front consisting of two round-headed arches. This survived the restoration, but the painting is slightly misleading. What looks like a course of white stone blocks at the top is the leading edge of a white altar cloth, and the arcaded structure below is made of wood. The altar top is a large rectangular stone slab, with five small crosses carved into its upper surface. This heavy top is supported on a stoutly built oak table with massive front legs that mimic the design of the wooden arcade columns: they are oak and octagonal in section.

The chancel as it was in February 1866.

The brass plates on each side of the east window (J05, J06, J07) were evidently already in place by 1866.

The view from the north-west towards the chancel shows that the medieval chancel arch was much lower than the post-1866 arch. The apex of the medieval arch was in fact only half the height of the 1866-67 arch. The original chancel ceiling was also substantially lower, with a series of horizontal roof beams crossing the chancel only a little above the level of the low chancel arch. The post-restoration chancel roof is lofty and made in the shape of a polygonal barrel vault. To go with these significant changes to the chancel there was a change also in the architectural design of the east window. The late medieval east window was a simple triple window consisting of a set of three equal-height windows with clover-leaf tops, set side by side and separated by stone mullions, within a rectangular stone frame.

A photograph of the nave and south aisle, taken in the 1860s.

Most of the window was made of square or rectangular panes of plain clear glass. The slightly irregular coloured inset panels look as if they have been recycled from a still earlier stained glass window. The painting shows that they included patches of red. At the centre of the composition was a red cross within a lozenge.

The 1866-67 redesigned east window has two equal-height windows with clover-leaf tops, set within a lofty Gothic stone frame that rises to a point. Above the two equal-height windows there is an arrangement of small trefoil and teardrop windows and at the top in the centre a cinquefoil window. The Victorian window is an altogether grander and very typically nineteenth

The old east window: a sketch reconstruction based on the pre-restoration photograph and painting.

century replacement. The early modern window was homelier, and perhaps more appropriate to a small village church. It also had quite a lot of plain glass, which would have let in more light.

At the eastern end of the south aisle there is now no window at all but a filled-in Gothic arch with a door into the vestry. This replaced a double window within a square stone frame, approximately matching the pre-restoration east window of the chancel.

As far as can be judged from the paintings, the wooden columns and braces separating the nave from the south aisle faithfully reproduce the late-medieval originals.

The 1867 east window

The horizontal beams crossing the nave also reproduce the medieval originals, as do the king-posts that rise from their central points to support the roof-ridge. Today, curved braces sprout from a point two-thirds of the way up the king-post to support the roof timbers. One of the paintings shows the medieval braces seated directly on the horizontal beams. The west wall of the nave had no west window, so the interior must always have been fairly dark. A large west window, fitted with plain glass and a sill down near floor level, might have rectified this by letting in the afternoon sun. Enlarging the area of the painting depicting the centre of the wall shows that there were two large mural monuments attached to it.

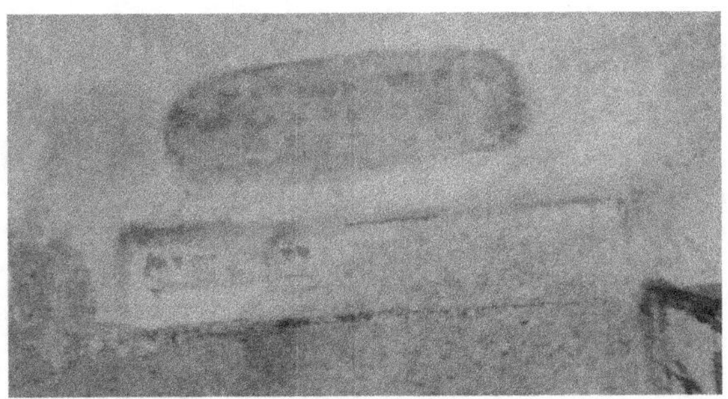

Two lost mural monuments on the west wall of the nave.

The watercolour image is indistinct, but it certainly shows two shallow but wide monuments.

The upper one was oval, the lower one was wider and rectangular. Both of them bore inscriptions. The artist has sketched four lines of writing on the upper monument, and three or four lines on the lower one. The pre-1866 photo also shows the two mural monuments; the upper one was a short oval, very nearly circular, while the lower one was a shorter and shallower memorial than shown in the painting. Interestingly it is shown as darker than the oval monument, suggesting that it might have been made of brass instead of stone. These substantial monuments did not survive the restoration and unfortunately there is no record of their inscriptions.

The medieval arcade separating nave from south aisle had a final wooden half-column attached to the west wall. In the restoration this was replaced by an attached stone half-column.

The original, much lower, chancel arch.

The medieval west wall of the nave had a substantial S-shaped wooden brace rising from near the base of the attached wooden column to support a wooden beam that was either next to the west wall or embedded in it. The earlier west window of the south aisle was similar in design to the one in the restoration.

Overall, the main difference between the 1866-67 church and the medieval church it replaced was the scale of the chancel, which was fitted with a loftier chancel arch, a taller east window and a loftier ceiling.

The reason why the sill level of the west window was pitched so high was that Ewan Christian, presumably working to William Parish's brief, wanted to include a west door – even though it was not a feature of the church's pre-1866 design. It was later found to be redundant and blocked up, which is how it remains today. But for the west door, the west window might have had its sill two metres lower.

The enlarged chancel arch, with the loftier chancel beyond.

The west window viewed from outside

The blocked west door

As far as possible, Ewan Christian kept to the original design. The main changes were the insertion of a vestry in the south-east corner of the building, the addition of a west window and a west door beneath it, and the substitution of a shorter broach spire. The pre-1866 spire, as shown in the Sharpe Collection painting of 1803, was noticeably taller than the present one.

The three pairs of windows in the south wall of the south aisle.[16]

The original broach spire

~

~ 6 ~

Through the Looking-Glass: the improving vicar

William Douglas Parish

William Douglas Parish was Selmeston's Victorian improving vicar, and it was he who was responsible for the complete rebuilding of the church in 1866-67.

William Parish was curate at nearby Firle from 1859 to 1863, after which he became vicar of Selmeston and Alciston. He remained there, living in Selmeston vicarage, until he died in 1904. He lived all his life in Sussex, apart from short episodes away at school (Charterhouse) and university (Oxford).

The Old Vicarage, William Parish's home

When he arrived at Selmeston, he was dismayed to find the church in a state of chaos. He noted in his copy of Gilbert White's *Natural History of Selborne*, 'Degradation of Communion Vessels. When I first came to the Vicarage at Selmeston and Alciston, I found that the only preparation for the Holy Communion (which was administered four times a year) was that the Clerk carried the vessels and cloths in his ordinary labourer's dinner basket, and set down the basket and contents in the corner of the Chancel for the Clergyman to arrange as he pleased. . .' [1]

Revd William Douglas Parish

He was both a neighbour and a friend of Edward Ellman, who organized and oversaw the restoration of Berwick church. Parish must have watched the progress of the Berwick makeover with interest, noting changes that he might make to his own church at Selmeston. Once Berwick church was finished Parish oversaw the restoration of Selmeston church, which he began in 1866 and completed in 1867. His restoration entailed the complete demolition of the medieval church and its rebuilding from the ground up. Today this would be seen as destroying the medieval heritage, but the Victorians saw only 'improvement'.

Parish became deeply involved in the work of the village school and oversaw its expansion. After the 1870 Education Act, he came to national prominence when he opposed the extension of compulsory attendance to voluntary schools. He wrote a pamphlet, 'School attendance secured without compulsion, an account of a plan of school management adopted at Selmeston, Sussex'. It was first published in 1871, went through five editions and was quoted in Parliament. Parish's scheme was to encourage school attendance by a system of cash rewards. Each child was charged threepence a week to attend. Parents of any child who completed 200 half-day attendances within seven months of the start of the school year (ie by May Day) qualified for a refund of two pence a week. Parents got a shilling back for each child who attended 400 sessions.

Parish was the fifth son of Woodbine Parish, a diplomat and traveller who amongst other things worked for Lord Castlereagh, drafting the peace settlement that followed Waterloo. The peace treaty signed on Britain's behalf in November 1815, the Treaty of Paris, was in Woodbine Parish's handwriting. William Parish inherited his father's wanderlust, yet – and there is a certain irony in this – he settled for the life of a parson in a very quiet country parish.

Apparently for excitement, William Parish visited America during the Civil War (1861-5). He also planned to visit France during the Franco-Prussian War (1870-1) but was dissuaded from doing so by his father. Parish commented to his friend Ellman that he had 'plenty of money, so when he took a holiday he could afford to go where he liked.' This did not explain why he wanted to take his holidays in war zones. But he was right about the money. When he died he left £6,365, the equivalent of £740,000 today.

William Parish made some interesting comments on education. 'My early training was the very worst that could have been given to anyone. . . "Do not ask questions" was the rule of reply to every enquiry. "Ask no questions and you'll be told no lies," said my nurse.

Parish's friend Edward Ellman, Rector of Berwick

"Little boys should be seen and not heard," said my Aunts. So there I was, cut off from the first steps to knowledge, and taught that an enquiring mind was one of the special characteristics of a naughty boy.'

Parish was a fundamentally genial and inquisitive man who always wrote kindly and affectionately of his parishioners. At the same time he was surprised by their ignorance, especially of local wildlife. 'I try to learn something of the ways & names of birds, but it is not easy – for the country folk are surprisingly ignorant of nat hist and if one asks them the name of all but the commonest bird an answer is out of the question.' His housekeeper was frightened out her wits by a grasshopper.[2]

Ellman described him as 'one of the most genial of men – who possessed an ever-ready fund of humour. He has always been a favourite with all classes, and an amusing conversationalist.' Ellman tried to persuade Parish to contribute to the Clergy Widows' Fund. Parish refused on the grounds that he had already helped the cause significantly by not marrying.

He was fascinated by the Selmeston folklore relating to the cuckoo, which implied that the country folk believed there was really just one. The cuckoo was supposed to appear on 14 April, when the local people believed that an old woman took it in a sack to Heathfield Fair and let it out. People would say, 'I've heerd 'un. She've let him out at last.' But in spite of their ignorance, or possibly because of it, Selmeston folk lived long.

'June 1st 1881,' Parish noted. 'This evening I met an old man and his great-grandson going home from their work together. The man (Richd Fears of Alciston) is 86 years old – the boy James West – 13. In Selmeston old John Guy (F15) who is 88 does as good a day's work as he ever did.' 'In Selmeston during the years 1884 to 1889 there were six deaths of inhabitants whose ages amounted to 501 years giving an average age of 83 years 6 months. The only other deaths which occurred were those of two strangers, each of whom died in consequence of drink.'

~

Diversion to Wonderland

William Parish counted among his friends the writer Lewis Carroll, who visited Selmeston a number of times and stayed with Parish at the vicarage.

Lewis Carroll, mathematician and dreamer

It is uncertain how Parish and Carroll came to know one another. Although they were both at Oxford, where they might have met, they were at different colleges and they did not matriculate in the same year. Yet somehow they met and became friends. Parts of the *Alice* books are said to have been written in the summerhouse at Selmeston vicarage.

The Reverend W. D. Parish would have been known to his parishioners either as Mr Parish or as Father William, which will remind some readers at once of some lines in *Alice in Wonderland* written in 1865,

'You are old, Father William,' the young man said,
'And your hair has become very white;
And yet you incessantly stand on your head —
Do you think, at your age, it is right?'

Is it possible that Lewis Carroll was addressing his friend, the vicar of Selmeston, our very own Father William? Discovering that the vicar of Selmeston was a legendary character in Wonderland has its appeal, but one thing that makes it unlikely is that Parish was still only in his thirties when the book was published, and therefore not 'old' at all, and he was a year *younger* than Lewis Carroll, who was born in 1832.

The poem is in any case known to be a close parody of the poem *The Old Man's Comforts* written in 1805 by Robert Southey. The original poem opens with the line, 'You are old, Father William, the young man cried.' So we can be fairly sure the name Father William was borrowed by Lewis Carroll from the Southey poem, not from his friend at Selmeston. It may nevertheless have been a joke between the two of them.

A granddaughter of Edward Ellman's remembered that when she was a child she saw a *papier-maché* model in the dining room at Selmeston vicarage. It looked very like the picture of the jabberwock in *Through the Looking Glass*. She is reported to have said that when she was a child she never tired of being told by Mr Parish how this creature had been the source of inspiration for a character in *Alice*.

A variant of this story appeared in a letter to *The Times* on 14 January 1932. It was from the Revd Frank Morgan, who had been vicar of Selmeston from 1923 until 1930.

We are all familiar with Lewis Carroll's awe-inspiring picture of the jabberwock, but it may be news to some that this creature of his imagination was actually constructed of papier-maché in the dining room of Selmeston Vicarage, Sussex, where he often stayed with the then vicar. . . A present

The Jabberwock

resident in Selmeston has vivid recollection of being taken, when a child, by the vicar to look at the finished monstrosity.'

Another Lewis Carroll character had its origins in Selmeston vicarage too, the borogove, a strange bird which was also mentioned in the Jabberwocky. This creature was based on a stuffed bird that was sent to William Parish from South America. Along the way, the specimen was damaged, but Parish managed to rescue the bird's head and long legs and had them mounted for display on a stand. When Parish showed it to him, Lewis Carroll was first intrigued, then became infatuated with it. He incorporated it into the Jabberwocky and a picture of it drawn by Tenniel was included in *Through the Looking Glass*, a curious bird with a head and long legs but no body in between.

All mimsy were the borogoves (foreground on the right hand side)

Lewis Carroll's Alice books were a satirical commentary on the Victorian world, a world in which scientific enquiry was a major preoccupation. This included the 'nat hist' that was Parish's interest: the collecting and classifying of exotic plants and animals. The traditional cabinets of curiosities grew larger and larger. From his rooms in Christ Church College, Oxford, Carroll no doubt walked, gloved but never overcoated, up to the University Parks. On his way he would have witnessed the palatial Pitt Rivers Museum taking shape in Parks Road, opposite Keble College. This cavernous building rapidly filled with shrunken heads, fossils, dinosaur bones and stuffed specimens brought back by explorers from all over the world – including the dodo that twenty years earlier Carroll had made a character in *Alice in Wonderland*. The borogove was Lewis Carroll's amused take on the 'scientific' collecting mania.

The Jabberwock, based on a model perhaps made by Parish and Carroll together in the vicarage, was clearly a concoction, a fantastical being. The borogove, on the other hand, represents a real part of the Victorian world of science, a world where incomplete and wrongly reassembled specimens might easily be laughably misunderstood. The looking-glass world of the Victorians was both hugely serious and very funny, depending on where you were looking from.

Unfortunately William Parish did not write about his intriguing guest, so their conversations can only be imagined.

This benign and genial vicar never married, dying of Bright's disease in September 1904. He expressed the desire to die in his study surrounded by his books. To make this possible, his bed was taken downstairs into the study, and there he passed away among his books. It was said in his obituary that he possessed probably the finest collection of books in the diocese.[3]

William Parish's will survives, dated 25 October 1904. He asked for all his household goods to be disposed of by public auction, the proceeds to be handled by his executors, his brother Charles and his friend the Chichester solicitor Sir Robert Knight.

He left his brothers Frank, Charles and Arthur £500 each, his sister Blanche £200, the Diocesan Association £100, John Ellis of Mays (G14) and Robert Matthews of Alciston £100 each, and to each of his servants Amelia Simmon, Fanny Kencett and Peter Verrall £20 each. He also left sums to various parishioners: £10 each to Mrs Eunice Moore, Elias Graves, John Hylands (H13), Mrs William Westgate, John Rumsley (J12) and John Piper, and £20 each to Eli Boys and Mrs Isaac Moore. He left £300 to each of his executors, in acknowledgement of the trouble involved in executing the trust of his will. The residue was left to trustees, with the income from it to be paid to his brother Charles, while he lived, and after that to his nephew and godson Walter Woodbine Parish.

May-Day

Frederick Stanley Mockford

A later resident of Selmeston was Frederick Stanley Mockford. He was born in 1897 and died in 1962, when he was buried in the churchyard at Selmeston, in plot A23. Frederick Mockford was responsible for inventing the May-Day distress call. When he enlisted in 1915, he gave his occupation as 'clerk', and he served from 1915 to 1917 in the Royal Flying Corps. After the war he became an Air Ministry official, taking part in the development of wireless for civil aviation.

The telegraphic distress call 'SOS' was first used in Germany in 1905. This was not an acronym but a Morse code signal:

$$\bullet \quad \bullet \quad \bullet \quad \text{—} \quad \text{—} \quad \text{—} \quad \bullet \quad \bullet \quad \bullet$$

This Morse signal was simple enough to repeat over and over again if necessary in an emergency.

As a senior radio officer at Croydon Airport, Mockford was in 1923 asked to think of a word that could be used as a verbal radio distress call, one that would be easily understood by both pilots and ground staff in an emergency. As much of the traffic was between Croydon airport and Le Bourget airport in Paris, Mockford proposed the French phrase 'm'aider' (help me) which would be easily anglicized to 'May-Day', and be easily understood on both sides of the Channel.

'Help me' in French should properly be 'aidez-moi'. 'M'aidez' is almost right, but should properly be accompanied by another verb, such as 'il faut m'aider' (you must help me) or 'venez m'aidez' (come and help me). But in English none of these grammatical considerations would matter: we would just shout 'help'!

'May-Day' was quickly adopted and by 1927 it was featured in the International Radio Telegraph Convention. It had become the international distress call.

In 1930 Mockford joined the Marconi Wireless Telegraph Company. He moved to Chelmsford and eventually became Marconi's General Manager.

Frederick Mockford married Winifred Jaggs in 1920. Among their offspring were Owen (born in 1921), Patrick (1922), Laurence (1924) and Doreen (1927).

~

Frederick Mockford's grave is to the right of the straight path that leads us across the churchyard from the lychgate to the church door. This is a path we share. Along this path many of those resting in the churchyard must have walked on their way to church on a Sunday. Richard Rawden, the vicar of Selmeston in the reign of Richard III, walked along it to take his Sunday service. In the 1630s and 40s, Matthias Caldicott, the lord of Sherrington manor and one-time favourite of the dissolute third Earl of Dorset, would have walked this path during the Civil War. His descendant and namesake would have walked the same path to church during the Napoleonic Wars. William Parish, the Victorian vicar, would have walked this path many times on a Sunday accompanied by his six-foot-tall, unsteady, stammering but good-humoured friend, his visitor from Wonderland.

~

RC

~ Part Two ~

The Monumental Inscriptions

~

~ Churchyard Plans ~

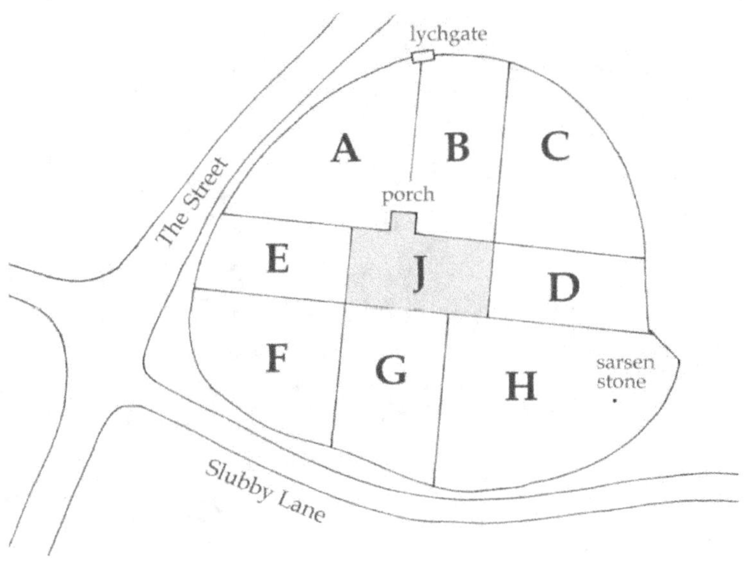

Selmeston Churchyard
An overall key to the plans. Sector J is the interior of the church.

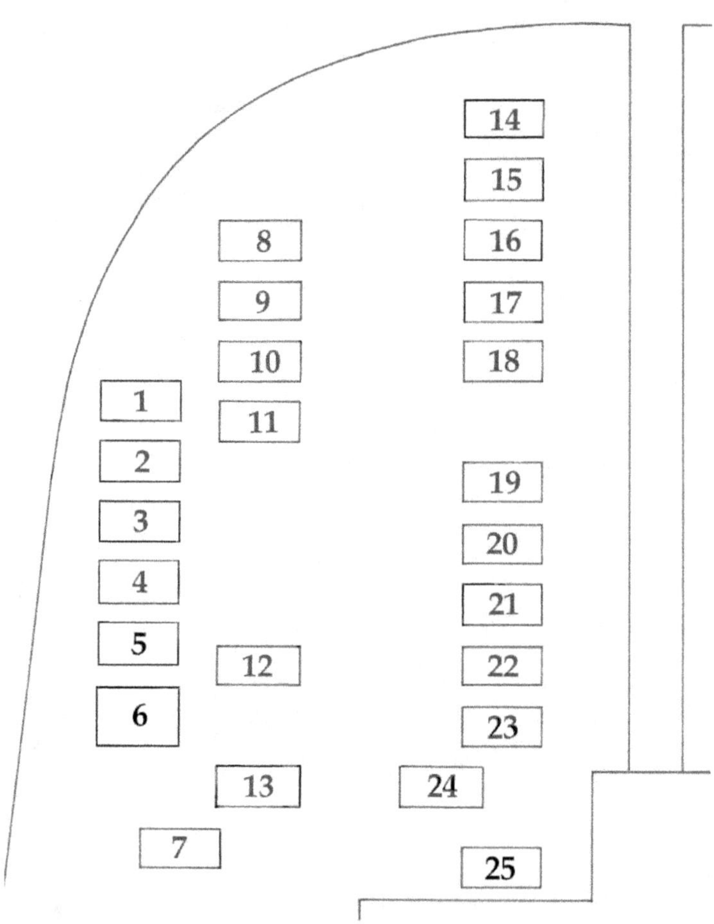

Sector A

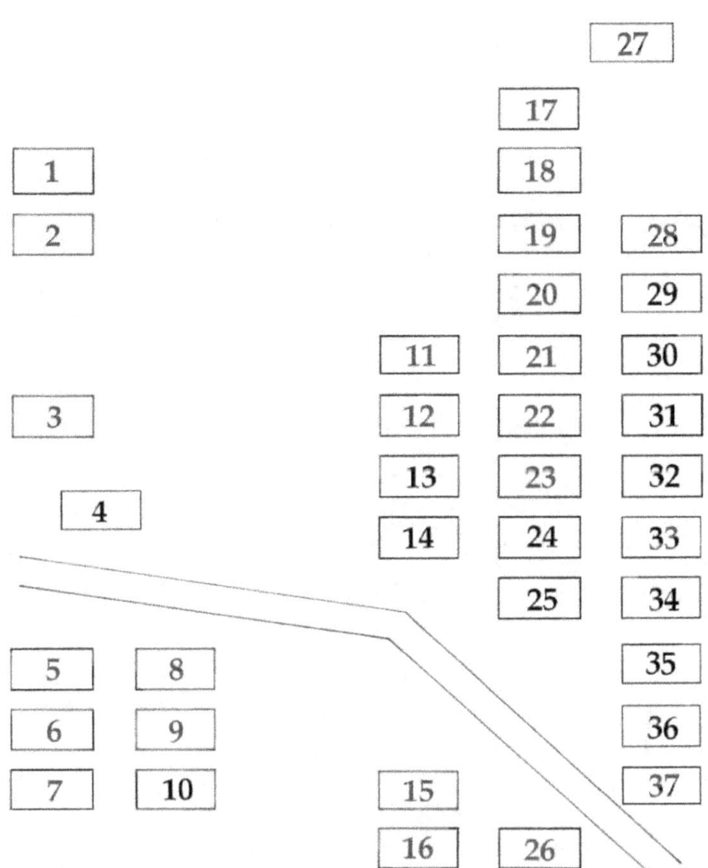

Sector B

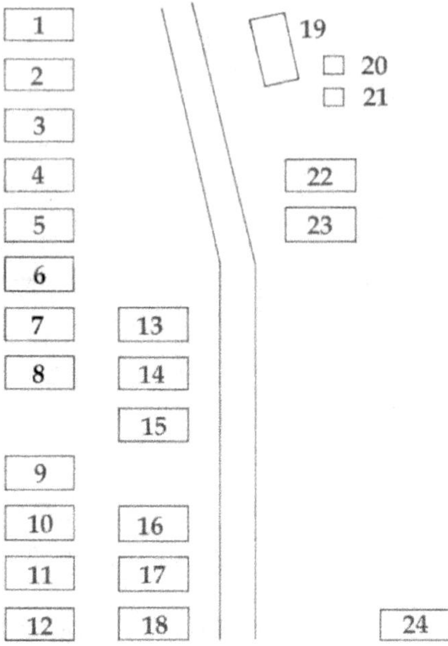

Sector C

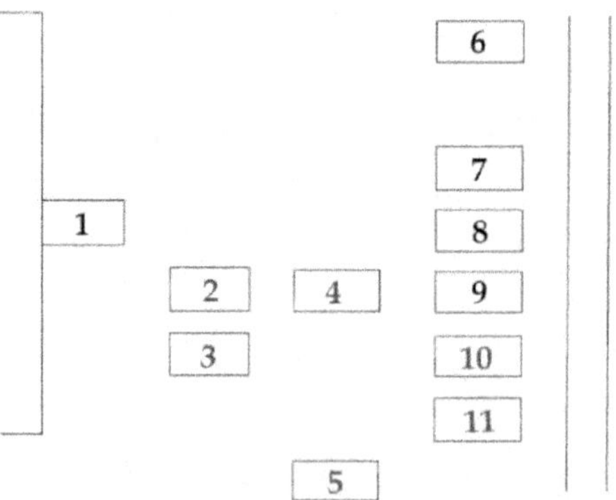

Sector D

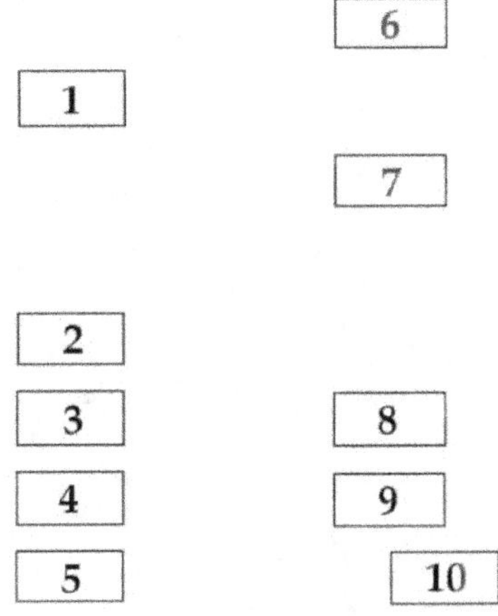

Sector E

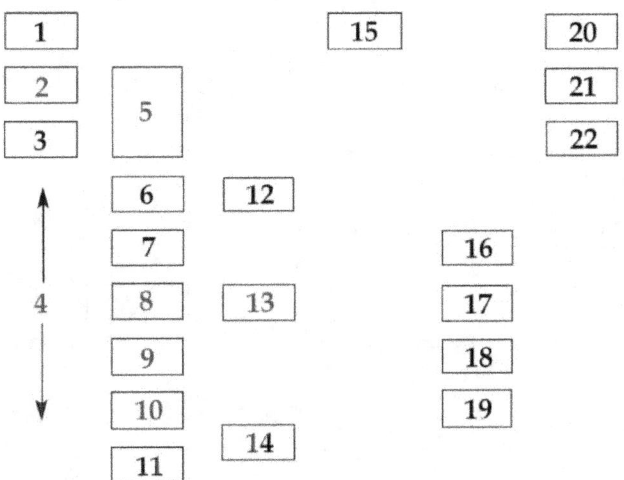

Sector F

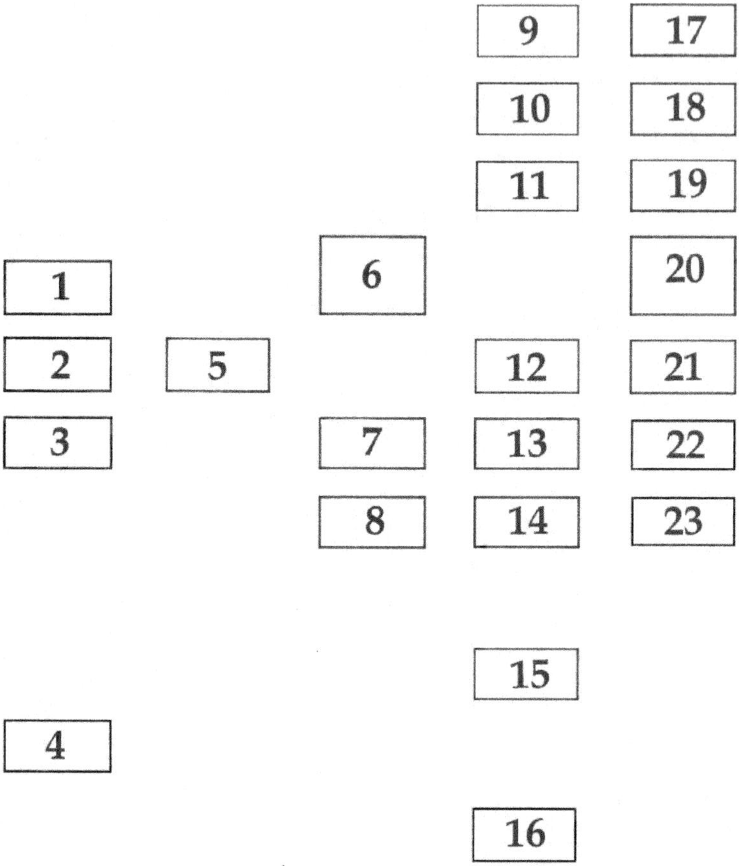

1

2 5

3

4

6

7 13

8 14

9 17

10 18

11 19

20

12 21

22

23

15

16

Sector G

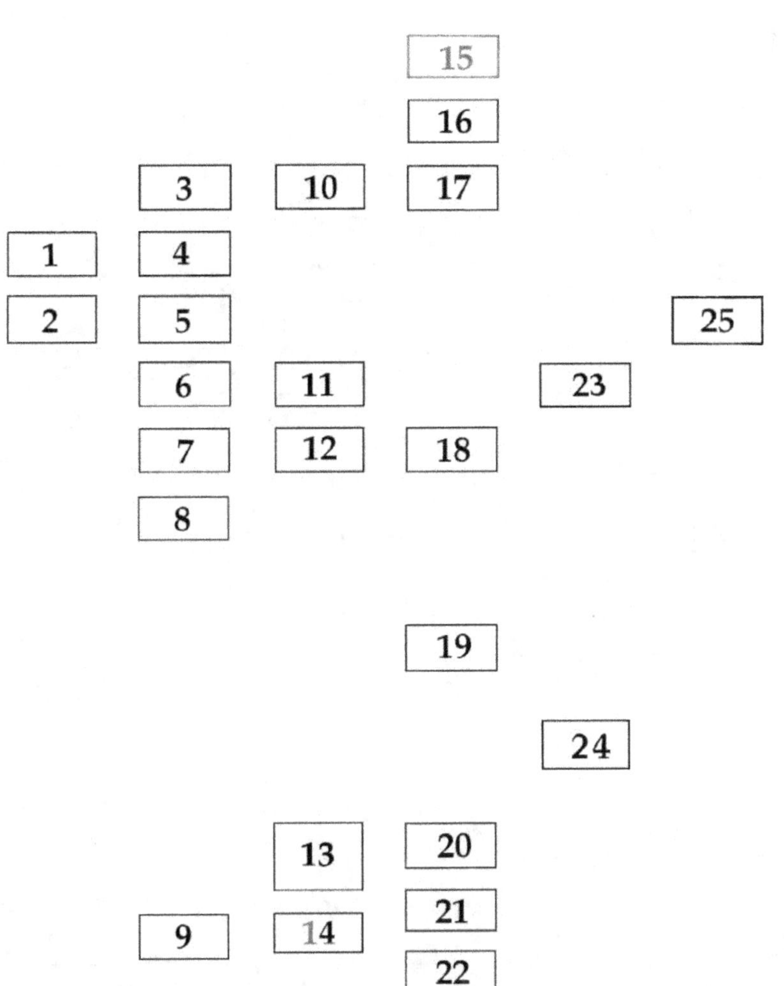

Sector H

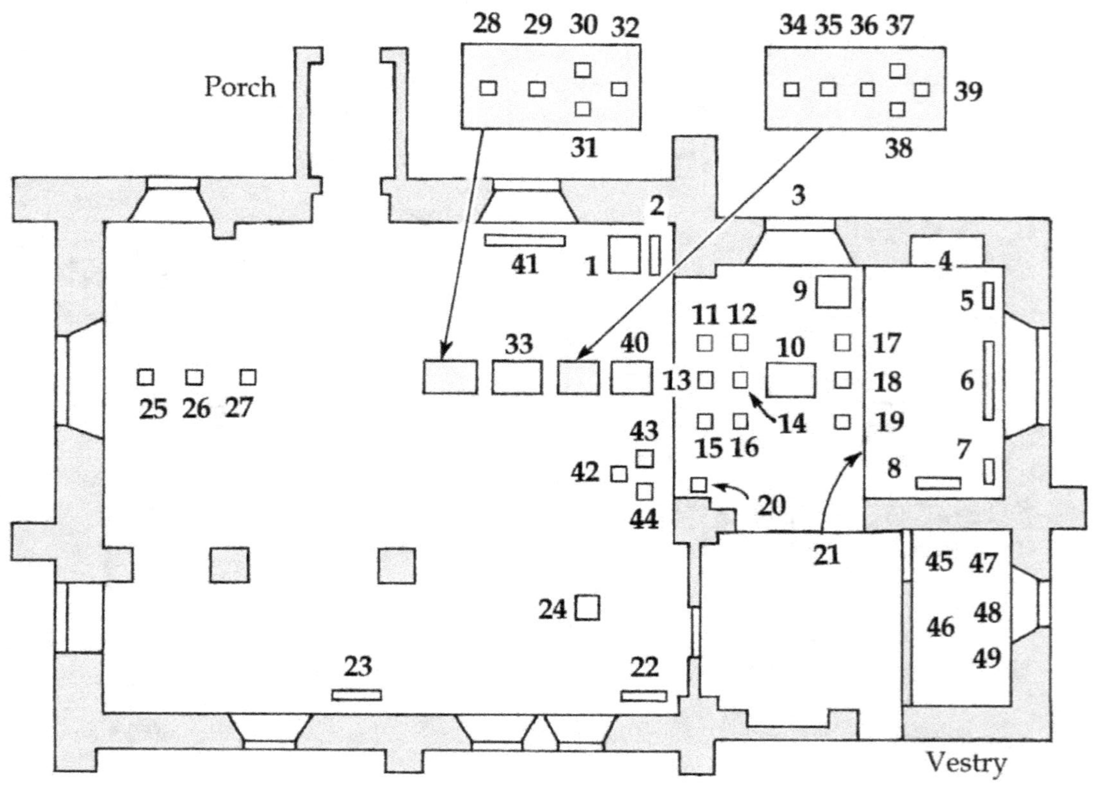

Sector J: Inside the Church

Plot A01   MOORE

MOSES MOORE

No inscription

No monument. Buried 27 December 1946, aged 86. Formerly of Selmeston, at the end of his life Moses lived at Hill House, Newhaven (PR).

Plot A02   EADE

ARTHUR EADE

No inscription.

No monument. Buried 8 March 1943, aged 69. Last address was Pouchlands House, East Chiltington (PR).

Plot A03   HUTSON

LUTHER HUTSON
& FANNY HUTSON

No inscription.

No monument. Luther was buried 3 February 1951, aged 82. Last address East View, Selmeston. Fanny Maria was buried 30 December 1941. Last address also Selmeston (PR).

Plot A04   HUTSON

EDEN HUTSON

No inscription.

No monument. Buried 17 July 1904, aged 67. Last address Selmeston (PR).

Plot A05   **HUTSON**

JOHN HUTSON

No inscription.

No monument. Buried 21 December 1899, aged 66. Last address Selmeston (PR).

Plot A06   **MOCKETT**
Headstone
Left hand side

In Memory of
HENRY MOCKETT
who died 2nd January 1853
aged 78 years

- - -

And of **ANN MOCKETT**
wife of the above
who died 28th Octr1796
aged 26 years.

Right hand side

Also of **HETTY**
second wife of
Henry Mockett
who died 15 August 1841
aged 63 years

- - -

JOHN FENNEL MOCKETT
son of the above
Henry and Hetty
who died 10th June 1848,
aged 27 years.

Footstone

H M	H M
1841	1853
J + F + M	A + M
1848	1796

continued

Double oval-topped headstone with checks and rounded shoulders. Matching footstone. Henry buried 6 Jan 1853 aged 79; last address at Firle. Ann buried 2 Nov 1796. Hetty buried 17 Aug 1841; last address Selmeston. John buried 21 Jun 1848 (PR).

Plot A07   HAWES
Headstone

Sacred
To the Memory of
WILLIAM HAWES
who departed this Life
May 2nd 1829
Aged 76 Years

Also of
MARY his Wife
who departed this Life
Janry 18th, 1830
Aged 82 Years.

Footstone

W · H 1829
M · H 1830

Peon-topped headstone with raised scrolled shoulders. Matching footstone. William was buried 9 May 1829, aged 75. Lived at Alciston. Mary was buried 24 January 1830 (PR).

Plot A08   COLEMAN

In
loving memory
of
GEORGE HENRY COLEMAN,
who died October 8th 1934,
aged 75 years.
At rest.

continued

Also of his wife
RHODA,
who died April 25th 1949,
aged 85 years.

Oval-topped headstoone with raised square shoulders. Shallow incised decoration on each side: Art Deco stylized roses on stems. Lead lettering. George buried 11 October 1934. Address The Old Poor House Cottages, Selmeston. Rhoda buried 28 April 1949. Address Meadow View Cottages, Ripe, formerly of The Old Poor House Cottages, Selmeston (PR).

Plot A09   MOORE
Top tier

In ever
loving memory of
NELLIE,
the beloved wife of

Middle tier

Henry **MOORE,**
who fell asleep
January 28th 1931.
aged29years.

Bottom tier

"Until the day break and the shadows flee away."
Song of Solomon Chap. 2. Verse 17.

Grey granite Latin cross mounted on 3-tiered stepped base. Lead lettering. Buried 31 January 1931 (PR).

Plot A10   MOORE

In
loving memory of
ELI MOORE
who passed away
Nov. 18th 1942.
At Rest.
aged 77 Years.

continued

Also **LUCY MOORE**
wife of the above
who died April 28th 1966
aged 98 years.

Fallen low headstone in rough granite, topped with raised square shoulders. Square topped kerb in rough-hewn granite. Eli was buried 21 November 1942. Last address 2 Old Town Cottages, Selmeston. Lucy was buried 3 May 1966 (PR).

Plot A11   BEDWELL

JESSE BEDWELL

No inscription

No surviving monument. Jesse Henry Bedwell lived at Selmeston: buried 14 April 1904, aged 43 (PR).

Plot A12   HAWES/ PIERCE

To the Memory
of **WILL. HAWES, Gent** who died
Nov. 10. 1761 Aged 47 Years

Also of **MARY** his Wife
who died March the 1- 1799
Aged 7- Years.

Likewise of **MARY** (daughter
of Will. & Mary **HAWES**)

And of **ROB. PIERCE** who died
Oct. 24 1771 Aged 27 Years

Low table tomb. Large rectangular slab resting on a brick base. William buried 15 Nov 1761. Mary, the daughter, not Robert Pierce, was buried 26 Oct 1771 (OBR). Mary, the wife, was buried 19 Mar 1799 (OBR).

Plot A13   NICHOLLS

**MARGARET JANE
NICHOLLS**
1899 – 1964

ERIC NICHOLLS
1899 – 1973

**SHEILA MARGARET
COWDE - -**
192 -
[rest broken off]

Low rough grey peon-topped double-width headstone with raised square shoulders. Square-topped kerb in rough granite. Lower part of the east-facing side, bearing the inscription has been damaged, so the inscription is incomplete. Margaret buried 15 August 1964, aged 65. Last address 22 Wivelsfield Road, Saltdean. No mention of Eric or Sheila in the PR.

Plot A14   CHILVERS

In Loving Memory
+
CHILVERS

FREDERICK	**ALICE**
WILLIAM	**ORPHA**
1874 ~ 1951	1877 ~ 1972

KATHLEAN	**STANLEY**
MILLICENT	**THOMAS**
1909 ~ 1939	1918~1972

FREDERICK	**ALICE**
WILLIAM	**ORPHA**
1874 ~ 1951	1877 ~ 1972

KATHLEAN	**STANLEY**
MILLICENT	**THOMAS**
1909 ~ 1939	1918~1972

continued

Oval-topped granite headstone with checks. Black-painted incised lettering with stylized flowers on each side. Pot stand in front. Frederick buried 15 November 1951 aged 78. The Manor Villa, Selmeston. Alice Onsha (sic) buried 6 December 1972, aged 95, at Eastbourne. Katherine (sic) buried 28 October 1939, aged 30. Manor Villa, Selmeston.

Plot A15   **TURNER**

In loving memory
ELIZA F. TURNER
7th Oct. 1928, aged 69

Very low peon top headstone with checks. Lead lettering. Eliza Florence Turner buried 10 October 1928 (PR).

Plot A16   **CROSS**

In Loving Memory of
DENNIS R. G. CROSS
01. 04. 1924 ~ 06. 04. 2014

MARIAN CROSS
07. 04. 1924 ~ 14. 12. 2014

Dear Parents and
Grandparents

Low tablet in white stone standing on white rectangular stone base, with pot-stand behind. Dennis Rupert George died aged 93. 7 Portsview, Portchester. Marian died aged 90, same address (PR).

Plot A17   **TURNER**

To the
dear memory of
JAMES EDGAR TURNER
25th February 1891
13th July 1968.
Thine for ever.

continued

Also his wife
ELLA TURNER
Née **OLDLAND**
24th January 1898
25th January 1982
Loved and remembered
always.

Low granite headstone, flat top with rounded checks. Lead lettering.
James buried 16 July 1968, aged 77. The Green House, Selmeston.
Ella Buried 3 February 1982, aged 84. 2 Fairfield Cottages,
Selmeston (PR).

Plot A18   TURNER

SARAH TURNER
& ROBERT TURNER

No inscription

No monument, but Selmeston Churchyard Register records burial.
Whose grave this is is nevertheless still unclear as there are two
Sarah Turners and two Robert Turners in the parish register.

Plot A19   TURNER

In loving memory
- of -
SARAH ANN TURNER
beloved wife of
Robert G. Turner
who died 19th Oct. 1924

Rough-hewn granite Latin cross standing on a roughly shaped
granite boulder base. Recessed panel on east side for inscription.
There is no Sarah Ann Turner in the parish register.

Plot A20   **TURNER**

Top tier

In
memory of
ROBERT WILLIAM

Middle tier

dearly beloved son
of
Robert & Sarah A. **TURNER**
died March – 1897

Bottom tier

Suffer the little children to come unto me.
Mark 10: 14.

Marble Latin cross mounted on a three-tier stepped base. Incised lettering. Robert was buried 11 March 1897, aged 11. (PR).

Plot A21   **MOCKFORD**

In loving memory
of
ALFRED MOCKFORD
farmer of Alciston & Selmeston,
26 years churchwarden of this parish,
at rest 30th April 1947, aged 85 years.

Also of his wife
SARAH WALLACE MOCKFORD
15th May 1950, aged 83 years.

Oval top granite headstone with checks. Lead lettering. Alfred lived at Alciston House, Alciston: buried 5 May 1947. Sarah Wallis's last address was 2 Downs Way, Berwick: buried 20 April 1950 (PR).

<table>
<tr><td>Plot A22</td><td align="right">MOCKFORD/ JONES</td></tr>
</table>

Headstone

+
In loving memory of
a dear wife and mother
EDITH MOCKFORD
who fell asleep Dec 5th 1959
aged 63 years
The day thou gavest Lord is ended

And of her husband
ALFRED HARRY MOCKFORD
who passed away March 4th 1971
aged 76 years
Together again

And of their daughter
EILEEN MAY JONES
passed away Dec. 13th 2007
aged 85 years
'Home again'

Tablet

**JOHN HENRY
"JACK"
JONES**
1921 - 2012

Square top pale grey headstone with checks. Stone flower stand and cremation tablet in front. Incised and black-painted lettering. Cremation tablet has maple leaf carved in top left hand corner. Edith buried 16 December 1959. 2 Downsway, Berwick Station. Alfred buried 8 March 1971. Berwick. Eileen died at Burdock St Mission, B. C., Canada. Jack died 8 November 2012 aged 91. Appt 403, 17528 59th Avenue, Surry, B.C., Canada (PR).

Plot A23	MOCKFORD

Left hand page

1st March 1962
In memory of
our beloved
**FREDERICK
STANLEY
MOCKFORD**
aged 64.
Air radio pioneer
and originator of
the distress call
· May Day ·

Right hand page

And also his
dearly loved wife
WINIFRED
who died on
12th October 1985
aged 88.

"Oh Lord in my
simplicity
suffer me to
come to thee."

Headstone in shape of an open book standing on a stone base with pot-stand in front. Inscription arranged on the two pages of the book. Lead lettering in capitals. Frederick's last address was Roxwell Road, Chelmsford; he was buried 6 March 1962. Winifred was buried 18 Oct 1985 (PR). See pages 86-88.

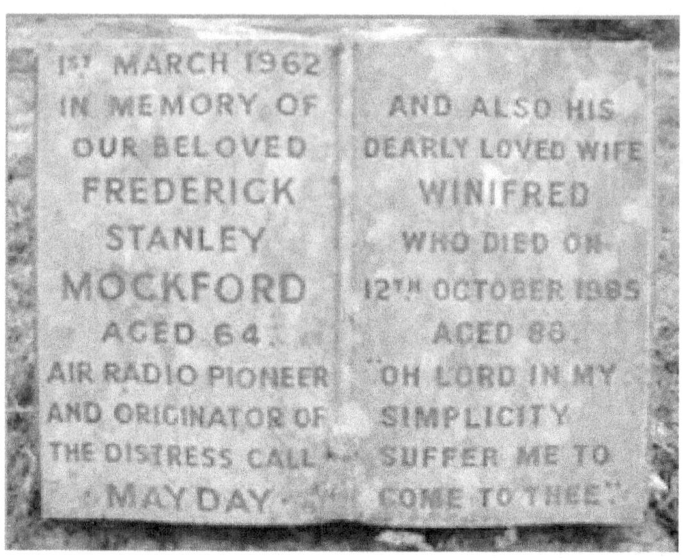

Frederick and Winifred Mockford's memorial (A23).

<table>
<tr><td>Plot A24
North side</td><td style="text-align:right">PARISH</td></tr>
</table>

REV. WILLIAM DOUGLAS PARISH,
Vicar of Selmeston cum Alciston

West end

and Chancellor of

South side

Chichester Cathedral.
Born 16 Dec. 1833. Died 23. Sep. 1904.

East end

"O Lord,
in thee have I trusted."

Large oval top ledger in grey polished granite. A large recumbent Latin cross is carved in high relief on the top. The ledger rests on top of a slightly larger granite base with ogee bevel edge. Lead lettering along the edges of the ledger. Buried 27 September 1904, aged 70 (PR). See pages 76-86.

The grave of Revd William Douglas Parish (A24)

<table>
<tr><td>Plot A25</td><td>CHILVERS</td></tr>
</table>

THE CHILVERS FAMILY

Wooden seat against north wall of church. Inscription incised along the front of the top rail. See A08.

Plot B01   **LEVETT**

In loving memory
MABEL ANNIE LEVETT
died October 23rd 1934

And of **TOM LEVETT**
who died July 7th 1951
At rest.

Square top headstone with square top kerb. Unusual asymmetrical projection of kerb on south side. Lead lettering. Two stone pots at the foot of the grave. Mabel Avril buried 27 October 1934. Last address Brambles, Pevensey Rd, Polegate, formerly of Cobb Court, Selmeston. Tom died at St Mary's Hospital, 123 Church St, Eastbourne: buried 7 July 1951 (PR).

Plot B02   **LEVETT**

In Loving Memory
of
TRAYTON LEVETT
of Cobb Court
who died June 15th 1901.
Aged 71 years.
Thou shalt be gathered into thy grave in peace.

Also of
CAROLINE LEVETT
widow of the above
who died Novr 28th 1922.
Aged 88.
Peace, perfect peace.

Gothic headstone with chamfered edges on west side. Inscription in leaded lettering on west side. Decorative carved roundel at top featuring flowers inside and sun's rays round edge. Trayton's last address Cobb Court: buried 19 June 1900, acc to PR. Caroline is not mentioned in PR.

Robert Stephens' memorial (B03)

<table>
<tr><td>Plot B03</td><td>STEPHENS</td></tr>
</table>

In Memory
of **ROBT. STEPHENS** who
died Sept 6th 1743 Ano
50 Years of his Age.

"O Lord,
in thee have I trusted."

Low headstone with elaborately scrolled top and scrolled shoulders. Carved decorative panel at top on the west side. The symmetrical design features a winged cherubic angel on each side. At the top in the centre an arrow points upwards to a skull. Buried 10 September 1743. All Saints, Lewes (PR).

Plot B04   SKINNER

JOYCE MAY SKINNER

No inscription

No surviving monument. Joyce May Skinner buried 28 November 1929, aged 9. Coney Hall, Selmeston (PR).

Plot B05   CALDICOTT?

- - - - - - - - - R - - - -
- - - - - - - - - C- - - - -

- - - - - - - - - - - - -

School - - - - - In this
Parish, - - - - who departed
this Life March 22,
AD 17-- ---

Large pale grey rectangular slab lying flush with the ground. Nos. B05-B10 are all laid edge to edge with one another as a group. The incised inscriptions are in poor condition and very difficult to read. Selmeston Churchyard Register identifies these six graves as 'Caldicott Family'. It also identifies another, unmarked, grave to the north of B04 as that of Joyce May Skinner. The Latham painting of 1846 or 1847 shows a row of three chest tombs close together on this site, each consisting of a large stone ledger supported on a plinth built of red bricks. These (the three perhaps standing for six) may have been demolished in 1866 to make work on rebuilding the church easier; the ledger slabs are now laid edge to edge, flush with the ground.

Plot B06   CALDICOTT?

- - -

Large pale grey rectangular slab lying flush with the ground. The surface is extensively spalled, destroying the inscription. Selmeston Churchyard Register: 'Caldicott family'.

The Caldicott tombs as shown in Diana Latham's painting.

<table>
<tr><td>Plot B07</td><td style="text-align:right">CALDICOTT?</td></tr>
</table>

WILLIAM Son of
M- - - - - -
C - - - - - - -
Anno - - - - - -
[blank]
[Also?]- - of - - - - - -
Brother of the above
- - - - - - - - - - - - - - - - - -
Which - - - - of December
- - - - - - - - - - - - - - - - -

Large pale grey rectangular slab lying flush with the ground. Almost completely illegible. SCR: 'Caldicott family'. Probably 'son of Matthias Calldicott'. William had four brothers: Matthias, Leonard (d in infancy), George and Samuel.

Plot B08   **CALDICOTT?**

- - - - - - - - - - -

- - - - - - - - - - -

- - - - - - - - - -

- - - - - - - - - -

- - - - - - - - - -

Mr SAMUEL C - - - - - - - son of

Robert - - - - -

Mr SAMUEL C - - - - - - -

- - - - - - - - - - - -

departed this Life M - - - - - - 1804 (or 1864)

Aged 76 Years.

Large pale grey rectangular slab lying flush with the ground. Most of the inscription is illegible.PR: 'Caldicott family', but no trace of a Robert Caldicott.

Plot B09   **CALDICOTT?**

- - -

Large pale grey rectangular slab lying flush with the ground. The surface is extensively spalled, destroying the inscription. PR: 'Caldicott family'.

Plot B10   **CALDICOTT?**

- - -

Large pale grey rectangular slab lying flush with the ground. The surface is extensively spalled, destroying the inscription. PR: 'Caldicott family'.

Plot B11   SPILLER

In Loving Memory
of
HELENA SPILLER
née Fischer
died 24th January 2000
aged 78 years.
Auf wiedersehen

And her husband
LESTER
died 10th July 2011
aged 89.
Bowled out.

Oval top headstone in grey marble. Incised and black-painted lettering. Incised and black-painted picture of a church (though not Selmeston Church) at top. Helena died at All Saints Hospital, Eastbourne, formerly of Lower Mays. Lester Walter John Spiller died at Inglewood Nursing Home, Hampden Park (PR).

Plot B12   SPILLER

In memory of
a devoted husband and father
WILLIAM JOHN SPILLER
died 19th July 1961
aged 64 years.
Thy will be done

Also of
LAURA MARY SPILLER
died 11h July 1976
aged 85 years.

continued

Square top headstone in grey granite, with raised shoulders. Incised decoration at top with tulips. Lead lettering. William lived at Lower Mays Farm, buried 25 July. Laura buried 16 July, last address 34 Hailsham Road, Polegate (PR).

Plot B13   WOODHAMS

In
loving memory of
**LILIAN ALEXANDRA
WOODHAMS,**
passed away 16th April 1965,
aged 62 years.

Small oval top granite headstone with lead lettering. Last address Willingdon, buried 22 April 1965 (PR).

Plot B14   LANGWORTHY

**BERNARD
LANGWORTHY**
17. October 1929
25. August 2010
A loving and devoted
husband and father

**BERYL MAY
LANGWORTHY**
10. November 1940
21. January 2016
Her words were kindness
Her deeds were love

Cream ogee top headstone. Stylized daffodils carved at the top. Last home of Bernard Albert Langworthy (died aged 80) was 2 The Cottages, Selmeston (PR).

Plot B15   BUCKWELL
Headstone

Sacred
to the memory of
GEORGE BUCKWELL
late of Tilton in this parish
who departed this life
2 May 1830
aged 56 years.

Also
SARAH BUCKWELL
Late of Tilton
widow of the above
George Buckwell
who departed this life
21st April 1851
aged 75 years.

Footstone

G + B
1830
S. B.   +   1851

Tall oval top headstone with checks and scrolled shoulders. The
edges of the stone are fluted. Matching footstone, and a rectangular
slab connects head and footstones. Incised lettering on west side of
headstone. George's last address Tilton: buried 8 May 1830, aged
53. Sarah's last address Walworth, Surrey: buried 2 May 1851 (PR).

Plot B16   PANKHURST

Sacred
to the Memory of
JOHN PANKHURST, Son of
Peter & Mary Pankhurst,
who departed this Life
4th December 1810.
Aged 46

----

continued

Tall oval top headstone with raised and scrolled shoulders. Matching footstone and large coffin-shaped slab connecting headstone and footstone. Incised inscription on the west side. Buried 8 December 1810, aged 45 (PR).

Plot B17 PHILLIPS

In
loving memory of
REGINALD PHILLIPS
died
14th February 1956
aged 73 years.
At Rest

Grey oval top headstone. Incised lettering.

Plot B18 BROMHEAD

MARY BROMHEAD
No inscription

No monument. Mary Elizabeth Bromhead, last address Cobb Court, Selmeston. Buried 16 April 1937, aged 82 (PR).

Plot B19 BROMHEAD

ELEANOR BROMHEAD
No inscription

No monument. Eleanor Bromhead, last address Cobb Court, Selmeston. Buried 11 January 1937, aged 79 (PR).

Plot B20	THOMSON

DAVID WILLIAM THOMSON
died September 16th 1942 aged 67 years

And his beloved wife
MARY ELIZABETH
died January 19th 1943

Very low square top headstone with scotia shoulders. Square top kerb with low square top pillars at corners. Inscription is half-buried. Lead lettering. David's last address Upper Tilton. Mary's last address Upper Tilton Farm: buried 22 January 1943, aged 74 (PR).

Plot B21	ROBERTSHAW

Tablet

In
loving memory of
FREDERICK DIGBY
ROBERTSHAW
31 January 1934
31 August 2010

In loving memory of

Kerb (East)

Kerb (North)

HORACE ARCHIBALD ROBERTSHAW
of Selmeston Court
born 12th February 1870
died 27th March 1951

Kerb (South)

Also his wife **ELSIE ROBERTSHAW** née Ambler
died 28th September 1978

Polished green granite scroll-shaped tablet bearing inscription in incised and black painted lettering. Set within a chamfered square top kerb with pyramidal pillars at the four corners. Frederick's last address Isleworth: buried 31 August, aged 76. Horace's last address Selmeston Court: buried 29 March. Elsie's last address Parsonage Farm, Uckfield: buried 4 October 1978, aged 86 (PR).

<table><tr><td>Plot B22</td><td align="right">SPILLER</td></tr></table>

In
loving memory of
ROY SPILLER,
who passed away May 18th 1951
in his 26th year.
*"We cannot Lord thy purpose see,
But all is well that's done by thee."*

Also of
LAURA MARY SPILLER
died 11h July 1976
aged 85 years.

Low granite peon top headstone with checked shoulders. Painted leaded lettering. Roy's last address Lower Mays Farm, Selmeston: buried 22 May. Laura's last address 34 Hailsham Road, Polegate: buried 16 July 1976 (PR).

<table><tr><td>Plot B23
Headstone</td><td align="right">DAVIS</td></tr></table>

In
loving memory
of
MARY F. DAVIS
1888 – 1953
At rest

HAROLD A. DAVIS
1895 – 1972

Square top headstone in white marble, with checked shoulders. Square top kerb, no pillars. Incised lettering. Mary Florence Davis's last address Culverake, Selmeston: buried 12 January 1953, aged 64. Harold Arthur Davis buried 15 February 1972, aged 77 (PR).

<hr>

Plot B24   MIDDLETON

**ROBERT DAVERSON
MIDDLETON**
a devoted husband
1905 - 1988
aged 83 years.
Thy will be done

And his dear wife
MARY (PAT)
1906 – 1992

Oval top marble headstone. Incised lettering. Robert Davidson (according to PR) Middleton's last address Coney Hall Cottages, Selmeston: buried 14 April 1988, aged 83 (acc to BR). Mary's last address 7 Coney Hall Cottages: buried 14 February 1992, aged 85 (PR).

<hr>

Plot B25   PIKE

In
loving memory
of
MARGARET PIKE
1922 ~ 2012

Oval top headstone in white marble with check shoulders. Incised grey painted lettering. Buried 16 April 2012, aged 89 (PR).

<hr>

Plot B26   PANKHURST

In Memory of
PETER PANKHURST
late of this *Parish* who departed
this life October the 30th
1791 aged 61 years.

continued

Also
of **MARY** his Wife
who departed this life July
[- - - the rest of the inscription
is buried and inaccessible]

Book-shaped headstone with raised scroll shoulders. Incised lettering. Peter <u>Panchurst</u> buried 3 November 1791 (acc to PR). Mary <u>Panchurst</u>, widow of Peter, buried 11 July 1793 (PR).

Plot B27   CHANDLESS
Slab

To the treasured memory of
An adored husband and father
**CECIL THOMAS
CHANDLESS CHANDLESS**
born August 2nd 1885
died January 24th 1958

And to his
equally adored wife
HENRIETTE
born August 5th 1899
died December 14th 1982

Base

Also their daughter
MARYSE CECIL
died December 9th 1987

Dark grey granite slab mounted on a granite base, covering a vault. Urns standing on the eastern corners of the base. Lead lettering. Latin cross carved in relief at the top.PR gives <u>Basil</u> Thomas Chandless as buried 28 January 1958. Henriette Aurelia Josephine Geraldine's last address was Sherington Manor, Selmeston: buried 21 December 1982 aged 83 (PR).

Plot B28   FUNNELL

ESTHER FUNNELL

No inscription

No monument. PR gives two Esther Funnells: 1) lived at Crossways, Selmeston, buried 24 February 1942, aged 76, 2) lived at Polegate, buried 10 April 1972, aged 75. Unclear which Esther lies in this grave.

Plot B29   FUNNELL

GEORGE THOMAS FUNNELL

No inscription

No monument. George's last address was No. 27 Alciston: buried 10 February 1949, aged 87 (PR).

Plot B30   GOULD

In Loving Memory of
My Dear Husband
GUSTAVUS WILLIAM CHARLES GOULD
who died 10th January 1946
aged 54 years.

Low square top headstone with checked shoulders. Raised panel with incised and leaded lettering. Decorative foliate panels top right and left. Square top kerb with square top pillars at the eastern end. Last address Lower Tilton Farm, Selmeston (PR)

Plot B31   WILDBORE

+
EDWARD WILLIAM REDSTONE
WILDBORE
1889 ~ 1972

Low oval top granite headstone. Incised lettering. No mention in PR.

<table><tr><td>Plot B32
LH page</td><td align="right">MARCHANT</td></tr></table>

In
loving memory
of
**DANIEL
MARCHANT**
who passed on
30th of Aug. 1948
aged 76.

RH page

Also
his beloved wife
**ANNIE M.
MARCHANT**
who passed on
5th March 1950
aged 86.

Reclining open book headstone. Incised lettering. Not Daniel but
<u>Samuel</u> Marchant buried 2 September 1948, aged 76 (acc to PR).
Annie Martha Marchant's last address Church Farm, Selmeston,
buried 8 March 1950, aged 86 (PR).

<table><tr><td>Plot B33</td><td align="right">MARCHANT</td></tr></table>

In loving memory
of
BESSIE MARCHANT
who died Sept 4th 1974
aged 70 years.

And her husband
WALTER MARCHANT
who died Oct. 18th 1988
aged 89 years.

continued

Square top granite headstone with rounded shoulders. Lead lettering. Bessie's last address Chebbles, Selmeston: buried 10 September 1974. Walter's last address Church Farm, Selmeston: buried 24 October 1988 (PR).

Plot B34   MARCHANT

**ANNIE HARRIET
MARCHANT**
died
1st September1979
aged 77 years.

Small square headstone. Incised and leaded lettering. Buried on 5 September 1979 (PR).

Plot B35   OLDLAND
East kerb

In loving memory of

North kerb

ALBERT ERNEST OLDLAND 1875 - 1953

Chamfered granite kerb with pyramidal pillars at corners. Granite potstand at western end of grave. Leaded inscription on E and N kerb. Albert's last address New Church Road, Hove: buried 28 October 1953, aged 78 (PR).

Plot B36   SMITH

In loving memory of
EDWARD PERCY SMITH
1891 – 1968
(Edward Percy, playwright)
Member of Parliament for
Ashford, Kent, 1943 – 1950.

continued

Wide granite headstone headstone with irregular curving outline. Metal plaque attached to the east side. Incised lettering. Edward's last address Selmeston House, Selmeston. Contributed to the screenplay for *The Brides of Dracula*. In 1934-35 he released twelve marsh frogs into his garden; they are now regarded as an invasive species.

Plot B37   TICEHURST
Headstone
LH page

DOROTHY SMITH
née Ticehurst
1911 – 1985

RH page

Resting
with
Mum and Dad

Tablet
Over the top

TICEHURST

LH page

GEORGE
1877 - 1955

KIT
1902 - 1992

**GEORGE
'DICK'**
1909 – 1993

RH page

KATE
1882– 1958

ANNA
1906 – 1998

continued

Below

BEATTIE
(Newland)
1912 – 1997

ALICE
1914 – 2007

Family together again

Marble headstone in the shape of an open book, with a tasselled bookmark in the centre. Lead lettering. Large square tablet lies flat in the middle of the grave. George's last address Hellingly: buried 25 May 1955, aged 77. George's last address Manor Cottages, Selmeston: buried9 July 1993. Kate's last address Manor Cottages: buried 26 August 1958. Beatrice Alice formerly of Fairfield Cottages, Selmeston: buried 27 September 1997 (PR). Kit, Anna and Alice are not mentioned in PR.

The grave of Helena Spiller (B12)

Plot C01A   **BUCKTHORP**

In
Loving Memory
of
VICTOR
'DICK'
BUCKTHORP
12. 4. 1914 ~ 24. 5. 2004

and devoted wife
MARJORIE
'MOLLY'
BUCKTHORP
8. 5. 1922 ~ 19. 3. 2009

New grave immediately north of C01. Ogee top cream headstone.

Plot C01   **TREGASKIS**

In loving memory
of
SONIA TREGASKIS
28. 11. 1915 – 3. 11. 2006

And devoted husband
PHILIP TREGASKIS
6. 3. 1921 – 22. 12. 2011

Low oval top granite headstone. Sonia and Philip's last address was Church Barn Farm, Selmeston. Philip Edward Tregaskis died aged 90 (PR).

Plot C02   **COWIN**

DAVID COWIN
5 · 1 · 1934 ~ 24 · 5 · 2006

VERONICA R. COWIN
28 · 02 · 1930 ~ 29 · 11 · 2017

continued

Square cremation tablet of pale stone, tilted. In front of it is a rectangular tablet with two badges representing the couple's service affiliation. Left is the badge of the Royal Air Force Regiment. Right is the badge of the Women's Royal Force. David's last address Rectory House, West Street, Sompting: died aged 72. Veronica Ruth Cowin's last address was at Woodside Hall in Hailsham: died aged 78 (PR).

Plot C03   **MITCHELL**

+

In cherished memory of
LOUISA MITCHELL,
who died 10th Jany 1957,
aged 51 years.

Broad low headstone, square top with check shoulders on the N side, low panel with floral decoration on the S side. Incised lettering. Louisa's last address Church Farm, Selmeston: buried 12 January (PR).

Plot C04   **CHURCHILL**

In loving memory of
ELIZABETH CHURCHILL
died 4th December 1948
aged 90 years.

And of her husband
SAMUEL JOHN CHURCHILL
Gamekeeper on Firle Estate
died 7th February 1950
aged 80 years.

Oval top headstone with carved oval panel at top depicting a pheasant. Incised lettering. Elizabeth's last address Tilton Wood, Alciston. Samuel's last address The Cottage, Tilton Wood, Alciston (PR).

Plot C05   CLAYDEN

LH page

In memory
of
a dear
wife and mother
ALICE CLAYDEN
who passed away
24th Aug. 1950
aged 64 years
God takes our loved one
from our home
[but never] from our hearts.

RH page

Also of
her husband
**THOMAS EDWARD
CLAYDEN**
who passed away
4th Dec. 1959

Headstone in the shape of an open book. Bottom line of inscription buried, so difficult to read; 'but never' is our guess. Alice <u>Clayden</u>'s last address The Lodge, Sherrington, Selmeston: buried 26 August 1950, aged 64 (PR).

Plot C06   ?
Vacant plot

Plot C07   **WILKINSON**

In loving memory of
ALICE WILKINSON
died 4th August 1959 aged 64

MARY WILKINSON
died 20th April 1961 aged 60

CAROLINE M. WILKINSON
died 25th June 1988 aged 91

BERTHA WILKINSON.
died 17th February 2002 aged 92.

Beloved servants of God and of this parish

Oval top marble headstone. Incised lettering. Alice & Mary's last address Fairland, Selmeston. Bertha's last address was Ringmer, formerly Selmeston (PR). No mention of Caroline in PR.

Plot C08   **WHITLOCK**

+
In Memory Of
WILLIAM FREDERICK WHITLOCK
died 18th November 1961
aged 73 years

And
STELLA LILLIE WHITLOCK
died 23rd July 1997
aged 98 years
Rest in peace

Oval-topped headstone with rough edges. Incised black-painted lettering. William and Stella's last address Church Farm Cottages, Selmeston (BR).

Plot C09   LEE

In memory of
HAROLD LEE
died 7 · 3 · 1965

&

MABEL D. LEE
died 16 · 10 · 1986

Oval top marble headstone. Incised black-painted lettering. Harold's last address Wannock, died aged 65. Mabel Davies Lee died at Southlands Hospital, aged 95 (PR).

Plot C10   FINLEY

In memory
of
FREDERICK
WILLIAM FINLEY
died 15th January 1968
aged 72 years

And
EDITH ROSE
FINLEY
died 3rd April 1951
aged 55 years.
Always loved.

Oval top marble headstone. Incised and black-painted lettering. Frederick buried 18 January 1968 (PR). No mention of Edith in PR.

Plot C11   ENGLAND

MARGARET RUSSELL
ENGLAND
died 23rd December 1969
aged 92 years.

Square top granite headstone with rounded checked shoulders.
Margaret's last address Hellingly; buried 30 December 1969 (PR).

Plot C12   WALTERS

In
loving memory
of
CLARE MAUD
WALTERS
28th February 1979
aged 91 years.

Oval top headstone in a hard blue-green possibly igneous rock. Lead
lettering. <u>Clarice</u>? (difficult to read in register) Maud Walters' last
address Selmeston House, Selmeston: buried 5 March 1979.

Plot C13   ROBERTSHAW

JOHN DESMOND
ROBERTSHAW
died 24th January 2019
aged 90 years

Newly dug grave with at the time of recording no permanent
monument. Small temporary marker.

Plot C14   WINTER

In
Loving Memory
of
CYRIL
STANLEY
WINTER
15 May 1928 ~ 30 March 2018

Polished grey granite headstone with rough-hewn edges. Incised black painted lettering. Maltese cross painted in top LH corner. Died 3 March 2018 acc to PR. Cyril's last address was Bowes House Nursing Home, Hailsham (PR).

Plot C15   NEGUS

BARBARA FREDA
NEGUS
16. 8. 1940 ~ 14. 6. 2014
A devoted wife and mother

Oval top marble headstone. Incised black-painted lettering. Projecting base holds a pot-stand. Last address Windover, Selmeston; died aged 73 (PR).

Plot C16   TURNER/ CROWSON

+
JOHN ROBERT
TURNER
19 · June · 1923
14 · September · 2010

continued

&
**MAUREEN GAY
TURNER**
Née **CROWSON**
17 · November · 1932
1 · January · 2017

Round top headstone in very hard dark blue-grey stone. Incised lettering. Incised Maltese cross at top. John's last address Campbell Crescent, East Grinstead: died aged 87. Maureen's last address was Hailsham House, Hellingly: died aged 84 (PR)

Plot C17   **TURNER**

+
**JULIAN
TURNER**
30 · March · 1933
25 · March · 2008
Loved son of
James and Ella
Much loved
brother of John
Pat and Jamie

Round top headstone in very hard dark green stone. Incised lettering. Maltese cross carved in relief at top. Last address 2 Fairfield Cottages, Selmeston. Died aged 74 (PR).

Plot C18   **LAWRIE**

In loving memory of
PATRICIA LAWRIE
née **TURNER**
10. 3. 1921 – 19. 12. 2003
Gave so much took so little

Oval top marble headstone standing on a two-tier rectangular base. Incised lettering.

Plot C19   **WOODHAMS**

In loving memory of
Mrs. L. A. WOODHAMS

Wooden bench with inscription carved along the top. Lilian Alexandra Woodham's last address was in Willingdon: buried 22 April 1965, aged 62 (PR).

Plot C20   **COTTON**

In Loving Memory
Of
**IVY ANNETA
THORPE COTTON**
Mother, Grandmother
and Great-grandmother
24th Dec. 1912 – 13th Dec. 2006.

Rectangular cremation tablet tilted up. Incised and grey-painted lettering. Last address was East Dean Grange, East Dean (PR).

Plot C21   **COOPER**

In memory of
**MARJORIE FRANCES ELIZABETH
COOPER**
a loving and much
loved mother
Died 3rd February 2003
Aged 95 years

Rectangular cremation tablet tilted up. Incised black-painted lettering.
Last address was Farnham in Surrey (PR).

Plot C22   WILMOT

**ROBERT
H W
WILMOT**
1944 – 2015
love alters not

Square top headstone with rounded shoulders and strongly rounded edges. Incised music stave runs horizontally across the top, and right round the back of the stone, as if to suggest that the music goes on for ever. Incised lettering. Robert Hugh William Wilmot's last address was 1 The Cottages, Selmeston: buried 30 November 2015, aged 71 (PR).

Plot C23   KENNEDY

1916 ~ 2009
**RENEE
KENNEDY**
carved out of love

Round top headstone with round edges. Large incised ankh symbol at the top. Renee Elizabeth Hattingly Kennedy's last address 3 Manor Cottages, Selmeston: buried 11 February 2009, aged 92 (PR).

Plot C24   COLEMAN

R · I · P
MAURICE BYRNE COLEMAN
1904 ~ 1992
loyalty

JOSEPHINE MARY COLEMAN
1916 ~ 2016
Trust, courage, love

continued

GEORGE BYRNE COLEMAN, D. F. C.,
1908 ~ 1945
Lost at Sea.

Round top headstone with checks and scotia shoulders. Carved
Celtic cross at the top. Incised lettering. Maurice's last address Little
Bells, Selmeston: died 16 October 1992, aged 87. Josephine's last
address Little Bells: died 7 January 2016, aged 99 (PR). George not
mentioned in PR: not buried at Selmeston.

Plot D01   **LATHAM**

+
Under this stone lie the mortal remains
of **MARIA** wife of the Rev Henry
LATHAM, M.A. vicar of this Parish
daughter of James Halliwell
of Cheetham Hill near Manchester
She died on the 8th day of September
1846 aged 50 years leaving an in- - - -
of the life of a true follower of the
Christ past in un- - - faith and - - -
ful hope and - - - charity. When the
ear heard her, then it blessed her; and
when the eye saw her it gave witness to
her: because she delivered the poor that
cried and him that hath none to help him.
The blessing of him that was ready to
perish came upon her and she caused
the widow's heart to sing for joy.
Job 29.11-13.

By the erection of a school house for the
villages of Selmeston & Alciston, a subject
which she had much at heart, her family &
friends have raised the most appropriate
memorial of one who was unwearied in her
exertions to train up children of her
poor neighbours in the way they should go.

continued

This grave is unusually positioned, with its head right up against the east wall of the chancel. A large rectangular slab is supported by a rectangular base and surrounded by a low wrought-iron railing, with three small iron crosses at the east end. Latin cross in relief at the top of the slab. Incised lettering. Maria was buried on 8 September 1846 (BR). The quotation from Job has the pronouns adapted: 'me' becomes 'her'.

Plot D02   GASSON?

Headstone

Illegible

Footstone

M · G   G · G
1802   1809

Headstone with an open book-shaped top and check shoulders. Incised lettering. Footstone displaced, reset against east face of headstone. Probably the grave of Mary Gasson buried 3 January 1803 and George Gasson buried 3 July 1809 (PR).

Plot D03   ELPHICK?

Headstone

Illegible

Footstone

E · E   M · E
1824.   1837.

Oval top headstone Incised lettering. Footstone displaced, reset against east face of headstone. An Edward Elphick of Beddingham was buried 27 April 1824, aged 61. There is also a Mary Elphick of Lewes buried 15 March 1837, aged 69.

Plot D04   **PARSONS**

In
loving memory of
ERNEST GEORGE PARSONS
died May 20th 1977
aged 75.

Low peon top headstone with checked shoulders. Incised and black-painted lettering. Base projects to make a pot stand. Ernest's last address Sandford Common Lane, Selmeston: buried 26 May 1977.

Plot D05   **SMITH**

In
Loving Memory
- of -
LUCY F. M. SMITH,

She died June 24, 1920
Aged 62.

Gothic headstone with bevelled east face. Lucy Frances Main Smith's last address Lower Claverhouse, Arlington: buried 25 June 1921, aged 63 (PR).

Plot D06   **JONES**

In loving memory
of
**GILBERT THOMAS
JONES**
20th Sept 1939 – 10th Nov. 2003

Much missed by all his
friends and family

Oval top headstone. Incised lettering. Gilbert's last address The Old
Poor House, Selmeston; died aged 64 (PR).

Plot D07   **MATTHEWS**

+

In Loving Memory of
KEITH MATTHEWS
2nd Jan. 1951 – 18th May 2001
A Big Man with a Big Heart

Oval top headstone. Incised and black-painted lettering. Projecting
base to make pot stand. Keith's last address was Glebe Cottage,
Selmeston: died aged 50 (PR).

Plot D08   **DENHAM**

**WINIFRED JOAN
DENHAM**
O.B.E.
Chief Officer WRNS
25th March 1908
11th May 1995
Dearly loved

Oval top headstone. Incised and black-painted lettering. Projecting
base for pot stand. Last address Croft Court, Seaford, formerly Rose
Cottage, Selmeston: died aged 87 (BR).

<table>
<tr><td>Plot D09</td><td>MOCKETT</td></tr>
</table>

In loving memory of
BERNARD GEORGE MOCKETT
died 11th July 1985
aged 61 years

and
TESSA JANE MOCKETT
died 9th January
aged 37 years

and
JUNE EVELYN MOCKETT
died 26th January 2018
aged 87 years
Together in peace.

Ogee top headstone in fine pale grey ?Portland Stone, standing on projecting base with pot stand. Incised lettering. June died at Deanwood Nursing Home, Brighton (PR).

<table>
<tr><td>Plot D10</td><td>SILLETT</td></tr>
</table>

In loving memory
PHYLLIS MAY SILLETT
died 13th March 1994
aged 74 years
Forever in our thoughts

FRANK RONALD SILLETT
died 2nd September 2000
aged 82 years
Sadly missed

Oval top headstone. Incised and black-painted lettering. Projecting base for pot stand. Phyllis's last address Willingdon & Silletts Restaurant (PR). PR does not mention Frank.

Plot D11	JONES

Headstone

In Memory of
ROBERT THOMAS HAWES.
Late of Alciston
who departed this life
5 May 1817.
Aged 58 Years.
So teach us to number our days that we
may apply our hearts unto wisdom
XC Psalm 12 verse

Footstone

R · T · H
1817

Double-ogee top headstone with check and scotia shoulders. Footstone displaced, reset against east face of headstone. Incised lettering. The quote is from the King James version of Psalm 90, Verse 12. Robert's last address Alciston. Buried 11 May 1847, aged 59 (PR).

Plot E01	HOCKHAM/ GUTSELL

In loving memory of
JOHN HOCKHAM
died 12th January, 1892
aged 76 years.

-

Also of **RUTH**
beloved wife of the above
died 30th October 1848
aged 30 years.

-

Also of **ELIZABETH GUTSELL**
sister of the above
died 15th May 1898
aged 74 years

-

continued

Also of **GEORGE**
eldest son of the above
John and Ruth **HOCKHAM**
died 5th June 1898
aged 56 years
They rest from their labour

Square top headstone with bevelled shoulders. Incised lettering which is very difficult to read because of weathering and heavy lichen growth. The stone is spalling. The surface bearing the inscription is hollow, and likely to fall off; then the inscription will be completely lost. John was buried 16 January 1892. Ruth was buried 1 November 1848, aged 30. Elizabeth was buried 19 May 1898, aged 74. George was buried 8 June 1898, aged 56 (PR). All lived at Selmeston.

View of the church and churchyard from the east, with
Slubby Lane in the foreground and the rectory in the background to
the right. The photograph was taken in about 1900.

Plot E02   **BOYS**

To the
Memory of
THOMAS BOYS
who died Novr 21 1867
aged 75 years

Also of **JOHN** son of the above
who died May 1st 1869
aged 39 years.

-

Round top headstone with check and scotia shoulders and footstone.
Incised lettering. Thomas buried 28 November 1867; last address
Brighton. John's last address 25 Hill St, Berkely Square, London;
buried 22 July 1869, aged 39 (PR).

Plot E03   **NEWMAN**

In Memory of **CAROLINE** the beloved Wife of
Elias **NEWMAN** of this Parish,
who departed this life 13th October 1858
Aged 38 Years.
I sought the Lord and he heard me, and delivered me from all my fears.

Peon top ledger with gable ends on supporting slab. Decorative rib
runs along the top. The gable ends are carved with tracery like
medieval church windows. Incised lettering in a Victorian version of
black letter. Difficult to read. Buried 20 October 1858, aged 38 (PR).
Quotation from Psalm 34:4.

Plot E04   **NEWMAN**
North side

In Loving Remembrance of
ELIAS NEWMAN
Who departed this life May 2nd 1878
- - - - - illegible line- - - - -

continued

South side

In Memory of
MARY NEWMAN
The loved wife of Elias Newman
Who died 3 Dec. 1873 Aged 66 Years
Whom the Lord loveth he watcheth over.

Peon top ledger with plain gable ends on supporting slab. Decorative rib runs along the top. Incised lettering. Elias died in Brighton: buried 8 May 1878, aged 63. Mary's last address 28 Hastings St, Brighton; buried 6 December 1873, aged 66 (PR)

Plot E05   NEWMAN

In affectionate Memory of **MARY**
the beloved wife of Elias **NEWMAN**
and daughter of William and Mary Noakes of Eastbourne
She died on December 3 1873 Aged 66 Years.
- - - - - illegible line - - - - -

Peon top ledger with plain gable ends on a supporting slab. The decorative rib along the top is trefoil in cross section. This is a second memorial to the Mary Newman commemorated in E04.

Plot E06   CHANDLESS

In
Memory of
EADITH CHANDLESS
wife of
Thomas Cedric Chandless
born 15. Oct. 1873,
died 20 Feb. 1924.

Unusual headstone with steeply sloping shoulders, a return, then curving sloping sides below and scotia shoulders down very near the ground. This headstone supports an ornate cross; in each corner there is a horseshoe or perhaps a 'C' for Chandless. Lead lettering on the east side. Eadith's last address Little Bells, Selmeston; buried 21 February 1924, aged 50 (PR).

Eadith Chandless's memorial (E06)

Plot E07   LONG

East side
Top tier

In
Loving Memory
- of –

Middle tier

CECIL LONG,
of Sherrington in this parish,
who died September 30th 1899,
aged 78.

Bottom tier

Peace perfect peace.

North side
Top tier

Also
of his wife

Middle tier

JANE CHRISTIAN LONG
who died May 8th 1916,
in her 74th year.

South side
Top tier

Also of
Their daughter

Middle tier

CAROLINE BLANCHE LONG
who died June 5th 1950
in her 80th year.

Large garlanded Latin cross with 'IHS' carved in relief at the crossing. The cross stands on a three-tiered stepped base. Small flower holders attached on north and south sides. Lead lettering. Cecil buried 5 October 1899, aged 77. Jane's last address Selmeston House: buried 12 May 1916 (PR).

<table>
<tr><td>Plot E08</td><td>HUNNISETT</td></tr>
</table>

In
Loving Memory
of
ANN SELINA HUNNISETT,
wife of
William Benjamin Hunnisett,
who died July 7th 1924.
Aged 81 Years
"I heard the voice of Jesus say,
Come unto Me and rest;
Lay down, thou weary one, lay down
thy head upon My Breast."

And the beloved husband
of the above
WILLIAM BENJAMIN HUNNISETT,
who died February 5th 1946,
aged 87 years.

Gothic headstone with slightly overhanging shoulders and bevelled edges. Incised lettering. Ann was buried 10 July 1924. William was buried 8 February 1946 (PR). The quotation is from a hymn.

<table>
<tr><td>Plot E09</td><td>HUNNISETT</td></tr>
</table>

In loving memory
of
HERBERT HUNNISETT
1886 – 1955
"At Rest"

continued

The memorial of Cecil, Jane and Caroline Long (E07).

Also **HENRIETTA BIRD**
Wife of the above
1881 – 1957
"Peace perfect peace"

Low square top headstone with check shoulders. Incised lettering.
Herbert buried 16 February 1955, aged 69. Henrietta's last address
Lymington, Hampshire; buried 25 September 1957, aged 76 (PR)

Plot E10   **PHILLIPS**
Left hand page

In loving
memory of
RENWICK C. B.
PHILLIPS.
Born 16. July
1916
Died 23. Dec.
1966.

Right hand page

And
husband
CYRIL
ALFRED TOM
Born 5. Nov.
1911
Died 15. Feb.
1990.

Base

I cannot Lord thy purpose see,
But all is well
that's done by thee.

Low oval top headstone with scotia shoulders. Carved panel at top
depicting a rose and garland. Inscription below is on an open book
panel with central tasselled bookmark. Incised black-painted
lettering. Cyril Alfred Tom Phillips' last address was 48 Mary
Burfield Court, Heathfield: buried 27 February 1990, aged 78 (PR).

Plot F01   MOCKETT

In memory
of
DAVID MOCKETT,
died 29th May, 1924.
Aged 64.

Also of his wife
MARGARET JANE
who died 1st February 1937.
Aged 77.

"For ever with the Lord."

Oval top headstone with Latin cross overlapping it. Carved decorative floral panels top left and right. Lead lettering. Double plot surrounded by a narrow square top kerb with bevelled outer edge. David's last address was Railway Cottages, Berwick; buried 4 June 1924. Margaret Jane Mockett's last home was School House, Arlington; buried 5 February 1937 (PR).

Plot F02   MOORE
Headstone

In remembrance
of
MICHAEL MOORE
died 10th Dec. 1875
aged 65 years.

Also of
JANE his wife
died at Groombridge
24th November 1899
Aged 83 Years.
Faithful servants and friends to
Rev. W. D. Parish.

continued

Footstone

M. M. 1875

J. M. 1899

Square top headstone with expanded rounded shoulders. Shallow projections on each side make feebly developed Celtic cross. Matching footstone. Incised inscription on the west facing side. Incised Maltese cross within a roundel at the top. Michael buried 14 December 1875, aged 66. Jane's last address Firle; buried 28 November 1899 (PR).

Plot F03   WOODHAMS

GEORGE WOODHAMS
&
FRANCES WOODHAMS

Square top headstone with bevelled edge and expanded rounded shoulders, checked. The whole of the east face of this stone, bearing the incised inscription, has spalled away, leaving only a faint trace of the lettering, which is now illegible. It is identified in the Selmeston Churchyard Register record of burials as the grave (Sector 2:59) of George and Frances Woodhams. George lived at Arlington; buried 9 October 1889, aged 63. Frances also of Arlington; buried 20 March 1896, aged 69 (PR).

Plot F04   ?

UNNAMED

Row of unmarked graves continuing in the alignment of F01-F03 to the southern edge of the churchyard. These are the graves of infants (Selmeston Church Register).

<table><tr><td>

Plot F05

</td><td align="right">

BURGESS

</td></tr></table>

HORACE BURGESS
ALFRED BURGESS
ALICE BURGESS
THOMAS JOHN BURGESS
&
FRANCES BURGESS

Unmarked grave, a double or triple plot, for the Burgess family. Location shown in the Selmeston Church Register plan. Horace Eli Burgess buried 17 January 1882, aged 12. Alfred James Burgess of Alciston buried 2 May 1899, aged 15. Alice Mary Burgess of Selmeston buried 12 February 1926, aged 46. Thomas John Burgess of 250 Elm Grove, Brighton, formerly of Selmeston; buried 11 February 1935, aged 87. Frances Burgess of Selmeston buried 21 September 1920, aged 71 (PR).

<table><tr><td>

Plot F06

Headstone

</td><td align="right">

GORRINGE

</td></tr></table>

In memory
of
HENRY,
?eldest son of
Pennington ?Innes &
Maria A. **GORRINGE**
who died 17th Oct. 1855.

Footstone

H · G
1855

Low peon top headstone with slightly overhanging shoulders. Incised lettering, very indistinct in places. Matching foottone. The words preceded by question marks are uncertain, little more than guesses. PR gives a Henry Gorringe, buried 14 October 1855, aged 2 days. The dates do not match.

Plot F07
Headstone   **HARMER**

In Loving Memory
SARAH,
youngest daughter of the late
Henry **HARMER**, of Hole Farm, Wartling.
Died January 27th 1902,
Aged 64 Years.
"Thy will be done."

Footstone

S · H
1902.

Gothic headstone with bevelled edge and matching footstone.
Decorative panel of carved foliage. At the top. Recessed trefoil in
the centre depicting flowers. Matching footstone. Lead lettering.
Buried 30 January 1902 (PR).

Plot F08   **SMITH**

TOBY SMITH

Unmarked grave identified in the Selmeston Churchyard Register.

Plot F09   **BAKER**

In memory of
BERTHA BAKER
1895 - 1970
GEORGE BAKER
1894 - 1979
JACK BAKER
1925 – 1978
FREDERICK BAKER
1922 – 1976
DORIS BAKER
1923 – 2015

continued

Low ogee top white marble headstone on a rectangular base that projects in front to make a pot stand. Bertha Gordon Baker buried 14 July 1970, aged 75. Horace Herbert George Baker buried 14 March 1979, aged 84. Jack Baker buried 31 May 1978, aged 52 (PR). No mention in PR of Frederick or Doris Baker.

Plot F10   **BAKER**

West

South

In loving memory of

Our dear son **ROBERT BAKER (BOBBY)**
who fell asleep January 14th 1935 aged 5 years.

East

"Suffer little children to come unto me."

White marble square top kerb with bevelled edge. Pyramidal pillars at the four corners. No headstone. Lead lettering on the bevel facing outwards. Robert Jordon Baker lived at Fairfield Cottages, Selmeston; buried 18 January 1935, aged 5 (PR).

Plot F11   **BAKER**

In loving memory of
LESLEY BAKER
24 April 1950
11 June 1995

Low square top headstone. Rectangular projecting panel carved in the shape of an open book. Projecting base to support pot stand. Incised black-painted lettering. Lesley Kathleen Baker's last address 31 Windsor Way, Polegate; died aged 45 (PR).

Plot F12   **HOLLEBON**

RICHARD HOLLEBON

Unmarked grave. Richard lived at Fairfield Cottages, Selmeston. Buried 16 June 1936 aged 73 (PR).

Plot F13   ELLIOTT

JAMES ELLIOTT
died January 9th 1911.
aged 84 years.
"Where I am, there ye may be also."
St John 14. 3.

Double ogee top headstone with double-checked and rounded
shoulders. Lead lettering. James's last address was Fairfield
Cottage; buried 12 January 1912 (PR)

Plot F14   KITCHER

In loving memory of
**JOSEPH HAROLD
KITCHER**
7th July 1934 ~ 30th Sept 2007

**JEAN OLIVE
KITCHER**
28th April 1938 ~ 3rd October 2008
Always in our hearts

Low rectangular tablet leaning against a cube-shaped pot stand,
both mounted on a rectangular base. All made of granite. Incised
and black-painted lettering. Joseph Harold Kitcher's last address
was Walnut Walk, Polegate; died aged 73. Jean's last address was
St George's Retreat, Burgess Hill (PR).

Plot F15   GUY
Headstone

He
asked Life of Thee,
and Thou gavest him
a long life
even for ever and ever.

continued

In Affectionate Remembrance
of
JOHN GUY
who Died 29th February 1888,
Aged 98.

Also of
MARY his Wife,
who Died 29th February 1868,
Aged 65.
Footstone
J. G. 1888
M. G. 1868

Round top headstone with slightly overhanging shoulders. Incised inscription on west side. Matching footstone but displaced, resting against headstone. The eight graves in a row to the south of this are unmarked and unidentified in the PR. John buried 5 March 1888, aged 95 (PR)

Plot F16   MARCHANT

HARRIET MARCHANT

Unmarked grave. No inscription. Location of grave recorded in Selmeston Church Register. Harriet's last address was Church Farm, Selmeston. Buried 22 February 1906, aged 84 (PR).

Plot F17   PAGE

In
loving memory
of
MARY ELIZABETH PAGE
died 23rd July 1954
aged 80 years

continued

Also her devoted husband
ALBERT ERNEST PAGE
died 16th October1954
aged 84 years.
"Re-united."

Low shallow oval top headstone. Rough-hewn edges. Lead lettering.

Plot F18   SHARP

ELEANOR SHARP

Unmarked grave. No surviving inscription. Location indicated by Selmeston Church Register. Eleanor's last address was Applesham Avenue, Hove; buried 1 April 1950, aged 74 (PR).

Plot F19   SHARP

MARY ANN SHARP
&
JAMES SHARP

Unmarked grave. No surviving inscription. Location indicated by Selmeston Church Register. Mary's last address was The School House, Selmeston; she died at Princess Alice Hospital, Eastbourne, aged 66, and was buried 14 September 1916. James was buried 30 October 1919 aged 68 (PR).

Plot F20   HUMPHREY

In
Loving Memory
of
EDITH HUMPHREY,
dearly loved wife of James William,
who passed peacefully away May 4th 1921,
aged 49 years.
"Till we meet again."

continued

Also In Precious Memory of
JAMES WILLIAM HUMPHREY,
Husband of the above,
who entered his eternal rest
April 26th 1923, aged 42 years.
"Thy will be done."

Large round top headstone with check and scotia shoulders. Elaborate carved floral border. Lead lettering. Edith's last address was Rose Cottage, Selmeston (PR).

Plot F21   COSHAM

In
loving memory
of
WILLIAM COSHAM,
Died 22nd Oct. 1966
Aged 96 years.

At rest.

Small square top headstone. Lead lettering. Last address 69 St John's Road, Polegate; buried 27 October 1966 (PR).

Plot F22   WHITE
WALTER WHITE

Unmarked grave. No surviving inscription. Location indicated by Selmeston Church Register. Walter White is not mentioned in PR.

The grave of Edith and James William Humphrey (F20)

Plot G01   **ROBERTS**

In loving memory of
EDWARD WILLIAM ROBERTS
of Clapton,1892
late C.C. for Bishopsgate Ward
who died at Hellingly on June 5th 1897,
aged 78.
"Gone, but not forgotten."

Peon top ledger with high-relief recumbent Latin cross on top. The
ledger stands on a bevelled plinth. Incised inscription on the north
side, on the north-facing bevel. Edward's last address given as
lodging at Glebe Farm, Hellingly (PR).

Plot G02   **TURNER**

To the Memory of
WESTON TURNER died
5th September 1884 aged39 years
the only son of the late
William Turner Esq
of Clapton, London.

Peon top ledger with high-relief recumbent Latin cross on top. The
ledger stands on a bevelled plinth. Incised inscription on the north
side, on the north-facing bevel. Last address: lodging at Cobbs
Court, Selmeston (PR).

Plot G03   **SKINNER**

In Memoriam
JAMES SKINNER of Sherington, Gent.,
Who departed this life November 5th 1875, Aged 88.
"I am the Resurrection and the Life." John. XI.25.

continued

Peon top ledger supported on a bevelled plinth. This in turn stands on a broad black slate plinth with an iron railing round the edge. Leaded inscription on the north slope of the ledger only. Buried 11 November <u>1873, aged 87</u> (PR). See also J10 and J41.

Plot G04   HARVEY

HARRIETT HARVEY

Unmarked grave, no inscription. The Churchyard Register gives this plot as the grave of Harriett Harvey. Harriett's last address was The Barley Mow, Alciston; buried 15 April 1890, aged 61 (PR).

Plot G05   CROWHURST

In
Loving memory of
my beloved husband
HARRY CROWHURST,
who died January 25th 1935,
aged 59 years.
Love's last gift remembrance.

Also of his wife
LOUISA,
who died September 18th 1944,
aged 69 years.

Oval top headstone with rounded checked shoulders. Low-relief carved decorative panel at the top featuring a floral design. Lead lettering. Harry's last address The Old Poor House Cottages, Selmeston; buried 29 January 1935. Louisa's last address 8 Mays Corner, Selmeston; buried 21 September 1944 (PR).

Plot G06　　　　　　　　　　　　　　　　　　　　　　　　　**DENNIS**
Headstone

In loving memory
of
MARY DENNIS,
died June 4th 1934,
aged 20 years.

And
L. A. C. ERNEST DENNIS,
died in Palestine July 8th 1934,
aged 21 years.
God knows best.

Kerb (east side)
Also of their mother **MARY ISABEL DENNIS,**
died May 10th 1954, aged 75 years.

Large double grave. Wide grey granite headstone with leaded inscriptions on the east-facing side. Square top granite kerb with pyramidal posts at the NE and SW corners. Mary Dennis's last address The Grey Cottage, Selmeston; buried 6 June 1934. Isabel Mary K. Dennis buried 13 May 1954 (PR). Ernest not mentioned in PR because he died overseas.

Plot G07　　　　　　　　　　　　　　　　　　　　　　　　　**PIPER**

Headstone

In loving memory
**CAROLINE LUCY
PIPER**
(née Turner)
died 17th Oct. 1952
Aged 67

continued

WALLACE
PIPER
died 26th Feb. 1958
Aged 76.
of Wheelwrights
Selmeston.

Tablet

ROBERT
PIPER
18 · 11 · 1920 ~ 29 · 4 · 2015
Loved and adored
by all his family

Ogee top headstone in fine-grained grey granite, with carved roundel at top containing a dove in flight, carrying an olive branch. Incised grey-painted lettering. Square granite tablet in front of headstone. Wallace's last address Wheelwrights, Selmeston. Robert's last address was 18 Hastings Rd, Bexhill; died aged 94 (PR).

Plot G08   FOX
Headstone

In
Affectionate Memory
of
SIDNEY LOUIS FOX
who died November 19th 1894,
aged 25 Years.
Be ye therefore ready also. St Luke XII. 40

Footstone

S · L · F
1894

Double ogee top headstone with check and scotia shoulders. Incised inscription on west side. Matching footstone relocated against east side of headstone. Sidney's last address was Jevington; buried 22 November 1894 (PR).

<table><tr><td>Plot G09</td><td>SELLWOOD</td></tr></table>

SARAH SELLWOOD

Unmarked grave, no inscription. The Churchyard Register gives this as the grave of Sarah Sellwood. Sarah Elizabeth Sellwood's last address was York Grove, Brighton; buried 14 February 1959, aged 80 (PR).

<table><tr><td>Plot G10</td><td>FAULKNER</td></tr></table>

ALFRED FAULKNER

Unmarked grave, no inscription. The Churchyard Register gives this as the grave of Alfred Faulkner. Alfred Leonard Faulkner of Selmeston was buried 28 February 1959, aged 80 (PR).

<table><tr><td>Plot G11</td><td>FAULKNER</td></tr></table>

ALICE FAULKNER

Unmarked grave, no inscription. The SCR gives this as the grave of Alice Faulkner. Alice May Faulkner of 2 York Grove, Brighton was buried 2 January 1961, aged 75 (PR).

<table><tr><td>Plot G12</td><td>MARCHANT</td></tr></table>

Sacred
to the memory of
MARY,
the beloved wife of
Mʳ Charles **MARCHANT** - - -

continued

of Mays in this Parish
who died 1st Dec 18—
aged – years

- - - - - MARCHANT
[and three illegible lines]

Flat ledger resting on a high rectangular plinth. This in turn rests on a large low plinth. Incised lettering. Badly weathered, difficult to read. Shown as Plot 3:61 on the SCR plan, but without any identification. Not mentioned in PR.

Plot G13   MARCHANT

In loving memory
of
CHARLES MARCHANT
[the rest is illegible]

Flat ledger resting on a high rectangular plinth. This in turn rests on a large low plinth. Incised lettering. Shown as Plot 3:62 on the SCR plan, but without any identification. Not mentioned in PR.

Plot G14   ELLIS
Headstone

Sacred to the memory
of
JOHN HENRY ELLIS.
who died October 6th 1901,
aged 69 years.

Also of
FRANCES ELIZABETH,
widow of the above
who died October 9th 1905,
aged 59 years.

continued

Footstone

J · H · E
1901
F · E · E
1905

Round top headstone with ogee shoulders slightly overhanging the sides. Recess roundel at the top of east side containing IHS monogram. Lead lettering. Matching footstone.

Plot G15   **ELLIS**

In loving memory
of
SARAH ELIZABETH ELLIS
died 25th March 1916,
in her 81st year,
'She hath done what she could.'

Round top headstone with ogee shoulders. Leaded lettering. IHS carved in roundel at top. Sarah Elizabeth Ellis of Lewes Rd, Ditchling, was buried 30 March 1916, aged 80 (PR).

Plot G16   **BOYS**

RUTH BOYS

Unmarked grave, no inscription. The SCR gives this as the grave of Ruth Boys. Ruth Elizabeth Boys of Sherrington Manor was buried 2 April 1965, aged 90 (PR).

Plot G17   **FOWLER**

In
Loving Memory
of
**EMILY
JANE FOWLER,**
who died Sept 9th 1877
aged 21 years.

Very small headstone in the shape of a scroll resting on a lectern.
Lead lettering. Buried 13 September 1877.

Plot G18   **HOCKHAM**

In
Loving Memory
of
JANE HOCKHAM
who died July 23rd 1916
aged 81 years.
"At rest."

Very small headstone in the shape of a scroll resting on a lectern.
Lead lettering. Buried 28 July 1916 (PR).

Plot G19   **HOCKHAM**

In
Loving Memory
of
JOHN HOCKHAM
who died May 8th 1909
aged 61 years.

Very small headstone in the shape of a scroll resting on a lectern.
Lead lettering. Not mentioned in PR.

Plot G20 CORNFORD

+

In loving memory of
JANE LILIAN,
beloved wife of Boaz **CORNFORD,**
of Mays Farm in this parish,
who departed this life June 22nd 1931
aged 55 years.
Rest in peace.

Also of the above
BOAZ CORNFORD
died April 8th 1956, aged 81 years.

Double grave. Broad granite headstone, oval topped with checked shoulders. Lead lettering on a recessed panel with a raised Latin cross at the top. Jane's last address Mays Farm; buried 26 June 1931. Boaz' last address was Station Farm, Berwick; buried 11 April 1956 (PR).

Plot G21 MACKAY

WILLIAM MACKAY
&
ETHEL MACKAY

Only the broken remains of a large wooden Latin cross, resting on a square marble base. No inscription is visible, but the Selmeston Churchyard Register gives this (Plot 3:49) as the grave of William and Ethel Mackay. William's last address The Avenue, Eastbourne, formerly Tilton House; buried 11 December 1917, aged 52. Ethel Deakin Mackay's last address was 13 Arundel Road, Eastbourne; buried 7 June 1937, aged 72 (PR).

Plot G22   PIPER

PERCY PIPER

Unmarked grave, no inscription. The Selmeston Churchyard Register gives this plot (3:48) as the grave of Percy Piper. Percy lived at 4 Manor Cottages, Selmeston; buried 21 December 1948, aged 65 (PR).

Plot G23   PIPER

Miss PIPER

Unmarked grave, no inscription. The Selmeston Churchyard Register gives this plot (3:47) as the grave of Miss Piper. No mention in PR.

Plot H01   CORNFORD

**RICHARD JAMES
CORNFORD**
18th June 1937
29th February 1940
Baby son of
Boaz and Allen.

Ogee top headstone. Recessed panel bearing incised and black painted inscription. Richard lived at Station Farm, Berwick; buried 4 March 1940, aged 2 (PR).

Plot H02   CORNFORD

ELLEN CORNFORD
Wife of Boaz
16th October 1901
17th March 1991
a devoted wife
and mother.

Ogee top headstone. Recessed panel bearing inscription. Ellen lived at Station Farm, Berwick; buried 22 March 1991, aged 89 (PR). See G20.

Plot H03   **TURNER**
Top tier

In ever
loving memory of
my dear husband

Middle tier

WILLIAM THOMAS TURNER
who died Nov. 5. 1944.
Deep in our hearts your memory is kept
We loved you too deeply to ever forget.

Bottom tier

Also **ELIZABETH MARY TURNER**
died April 12th 1970 aged 92 years

Also their son **GEORGE**
died in infancy Dec.10th 1917

Marble Latin cross on a three-tier stepped base. Square topped kerb. Incised and leaded lettering on the east side of the stepped base. William Turner was buried 18 November 1944, aged 67. Elizabeth was buried 17 April 1970. George Alexander Turner of Ludlay Cottages was buried 5 December <u>1918</u>, aged 12 months (PR). The dates conflict.

Plot H04   **CALVERT LEE**

+
**WILLIAM GORDON
CALVERT LEE**
1898 – 1957
Vicar
of
Selmeston cum Alciston

And
his wife
**MURIEL EDITH
CALVERT LEE**
1904 – 1994

continued

I will lift up mine eyes
unto the hills.

Flat rectangular ledger with incised lettering. Calvert Lee was vicar very briefly, 1956-1957. Surprisingly few vicars of Selmeston have burial inscriptions in the church or churchyard: Henry Rogers, 1607-1639 (J24), W. D. Parish, 1863-1904 (A24, J03, J08) and William Calvert Lee. William was buried 11 September 1957, aged 59. Muriel's last address 4 Manor Cottages, Selmeston; buried 7 July 1994, aged 89 (PR).

Plot H05   CALVERT LEE

**EDMUND PAUL
CALVERT LEE**
1927 – 1990
Into his quietness

And his wife
ISABEL GILLIAN
1935 – 1995
At peace in our hearts

Flat rectangular ledger with incised lettering. Stone pot stand at head. Edmund's last address 142 High Street, Lewes; buried 16 February 1990, aged 63. Isabel not mentioned in PR.

Plot H06   CREED

In
loving memory
of
HILDA CREED,
died 27th July 1958.
Ever in our thoughts.

continued

Red granite headstone. Incised decorative flowers in upper left and upper right corners. Lead lettering. Hilda Rose Creed lived at Lullington Court Farm, Litlington. Buried 1 August 1958, aged 62 (PR).

Plot H07   **BROOK**

JESSE BROOK

Unmarked grave, no inscription. The SCR gives this as the grave of Jesse Brook. Died in Brighton General Hospital, aged 95. Buried 18 August 1955 (PR).

Plot H08   **BROOK**

EUNICE BROOK

Unmarked grave, no inscription. The SCR gives this as the grave of Eunice Brook. Eunice Brook lived at Twydown Cottage, Selmeston. Buried 19 April 1939, aged 61 (PR).

Plot H09   **WEST**

ELIZABETH WEST
& ALICE WEST

Unmarked grave, no inscription. The SCR gives this as the grave of Elizabeth & Alice West. Elizabeth Lydia west died aged 70 at Princess Alice Hospital, and formerly lived at Chiddingly. Buried 27 November 1947. No mention of Alice in PR.

<table><tr><td>Plot H10</td><td>TURNER</td></tr></table>

GEORGE TURNER

Unmarked grave, no inscription. The SCR gives this as the grave of George Turner. George Turner came from Arlington. He died at the age of 14 and was buried 20 February 1853 (PR).

<table><tr><td>Plot H11</td><td>WENHAM</td></tr></table>

Sacred
to the Memory
of
GEORGE WENHAM
died 31st December 1914
aged 82 years.
Interred at Hellingly cemetery

Also of **MARGARET** wife of the above
who died 2nd July 1874,
aged 40 years.

And of
ANNIE MARGARET WENHAM,
daughter of the above
who died 13th February 1870,
aged 8 months.

Also of
MARTHA JACKSON WENHAM,
(daughter-in-law)
the beloved wife of
Henry William Wenham,
who passed peacefully away
8th April 1926
aged 63 years.

continued

Tall round top headstone with round shoulders. Incised lettering. Square top kerb. Margaret buried 5 July 1874, aged 41. Annie buried 17 February 1871, aged 7 months. Martha, of Havelock Rd, Preston, Brighton; buried 15 April 1926 (PR). George not mentioned in PR.

Plot H12   **RUMSLEY**

+

In

affectionate remembrance

of

EMILY daughter of

John and Emily **RUMSLEY**

died Augst14th 1879

aged 19 years

"Blessed are the dead which

die in the Lord." Rev. XIV. 13.

Small square top headstone with rounded and checked shoulders. Matching footstone repositioned close to the headstone. Emily buried 17 August 1879 (PR).

Plot H13   **HYLANDS**

In loving memory of

CHRISTINA HYLANDS,

died Jan. 13th 1917,

aged 64 years.

Also of her husband,

JOHN BOND HYLANDS

died July 26th 1937,

aged 84 years.

"At rest."

Double grave. Low headstone in grey granite with square top kerb severely displaced on the north side by the growth of a tree. Stone pot stand on kerb at east end of grave. Christina buried 17 Jan 1917. John buried 2 Aug 1939. John's last address Old Town Cottages, Selmeston (PR).

<table><tr><td>

Plot H14

</td><td align="right">

HYLANDS/ STEVENS

</td></tr></table>

PERCY HYLANDS
1894 ~ 1929

BERNARD STEVENS
1919 ~2007

RHODA STEVENS
(Née Hylands)
1921 ~ 2009

Oval top headstone in pale stone with check shoulders. Incised and
pale blue-painted lettering. Percy buried 25 May 1929 aged 55: last
address Station Rd, Plumpton. Bernard Victor Stevens buried Feb
2007 aged 87: last address was 47 Montefiore Rd, Hove. Rhoda
Christine Stevens buried 19 Jan 2009 aged 87: her last address was
also 47 Montefiore Road, Hove (PR).

<table><tr><td>

Plot H15
Headstone

</td><td align="right">

RUMSLEY

</td></tr></table>

In
ever loving memory of
our dear father
THOMAS RUMSLEY,
born in Selmeston March 13th 1860
died in Clapham, Surrey
October 26th 1895
Then are they glad because they
are at rest, and so he bringeth them
unto the haven where they would be
Psm. CVII.30

Footstone

T · R
1895

Round top headstone with check and exaggerated rounded
shoulders. Bevel edge. Matching footstone. Thomas was buried 31
Oct 1895 aged 85; last address Selmeston House, Clapham
Common (PR).

Plot H16   RUMSLEY

Headstone

In remembrance
of
HARRIET RUMSLEY
widow of
Reuben Rumsley,
died 8th February 1867.
aged 76.

Footstone

H · R
1867

Low oval top headstone with check and scotia shoulders. Incised
lettering. Matching footstone propped against it on its side,
presumably to stop it obscuring the inscription on the headstone.
Harriet lived at Selmeston. Buried 14 February 1867 (PR).

Plot H17   RUMSLEY

In remembrance
of
REUBEN RUMSLEY
parish clerk of Selmeston
for 50 years.
Died 7th July 1863
aged 79.

Round top headstone with check and scotia shoulders. Incised
lettering on east side. Reuben lived at Selmeston. Buried 12 July
1863 (PR).

Plot H18   **RUMSLEY**
Headstone

+

In affectionate
remembrance
of
JOHN RUMSLEY
died 3rd April 1874
aged 2 years.

Footstone

J . R
1874

Low square top headstone with rounded check shoulders. Matching footstone displaced, leaning against the headstone. Maltese cross in relief within a roundel at the top. Incised lettering. Lived at Selmeston. Buried 7 April 1874 (PR).

Plot H19   **LEVETT**

THOMAS LEVETT
died Aug 22 1878
aged 37 years

Cast-iron wheel cross with a fleur de lys at the termination of each of the branches of the cross. Raised inscription on west side, arranged in a circle. Thomas's last address Eastbourne; buried 26 August 1878 (PR).

Plot H20   **HIBBS**

+

In memory of
dear father
REUBEN JOHN HIBBS
died 27th May 1921
aged 61 years.

continued

Low headstone with shallow wave shaped top. Originally lead lettering, but all the leads have gone. Reuben lived at Batbrooks Cottages, Selmeston; buried 30 May 1921 (PR).

Plot H21   OBBARD

In
Loving memory of
our dear mother
ALICE EMMA OBBARD,
died 26th May 1940,
aged 55 years.

Low headstone in the shape of a scroll on a lectern. Incised and leaded lettering on east side. Lived at Rail Cottage, Selmeston; buried 29 May 1940 (PR).

Plot H22   ENGLAND

GWENDOLINE M. R. ENGLAND
died July 6th 1956
aged 90 years

Square top kerb. No headstone. Sloping tablet with incised inscription as footstone. Large stone urn or bird-bath in centre. Gwendoline Mary R. England's last address was in Seaford; buried 12 July 1956 (PR).

Plot H23   MARQUAND/ REES

Rt. Hon. HILARY A. MARQUAND
1901 ~ 1972
socialist and teacher

continued

and his beloved and
accomplished wife
RACHEL ELUNED Née **REES**
1903 ~ 1996

Gothic top headstone with bevelled edge. Incised lettering. Hilary Adair Marquand lived at Grey Cottage, Selmeston; buried 10 November 1972, aged 70. Rachel died at Blenheim Nursing Home, Sheffield, formerly lived at Grey Cottage, Selmeston; buried 29 February 1996, aged 92 (PR).

Plot H24   **BROOKER**

In loving memory of dear mother
SARAH CAROLINE BROOKE,
who fell asleep April 10th 1913.

Square top kerb, no headstone. Lead lettering on top of south kerb only. Buried 13 April 1913, aged 59 (PR).

Plot H25   **TURNER**
Headstone

In
loving
Remembrance of
our dear sister
JANE ELLEN wife of
Thomas **TURNER,**
who died Sept. 6th 1886
aged 60 years.
In midst of life we are in death.

Footstone

J . E . T
1866

Unusual low headstone shaped like a *fleur de lys* with no shoulders but sloping sides. Incised inscription on west side. Non-matching peon top footstone, separated from headstone by a tree. Jane died at Lewes; buried 11 September 1886 (PR).

Plot J01   **ALLWORK/ CALDICOTT**

Here are deposited the Remains of
MARY, wife of Thomas **ALLWORK,**
of Seaford, Gent.
And Widow of
Matthias **CALDICOTT,**
late of Sherington, in this Parish, Gent.
who died 16th January 1831,
Aged 72 Years.

Rectangular white marble tablet laid flush with the floor. Incised black-painted lettering. The chancel wall oversteps its eastern edge and the marble plaque is broken parallel to this, showing that the wall was built over the marble slab, its weight breaking it. It therefore predates the 1860 rebuilding. PR says that Mary was 'buried in tp'.

Brass plate commemorating Matthias Caldicott, Gentleman (J02)

Plot J02 CALDICOTT

+
Sacred to the Memory of
MATTHIAS CALDICOTT,
late of Sherington in this Parish,
~ GENTLEMAN ~
who died 19th Feby 1808, Aged 53 Years.

Brass plate fixed to wall. Double-line border. Incised black-painted lettering with red initial capitals.

Plot J03 PARISH

To the glory of God, and in memory of the **REV. WILLIAM DOUGLAS PARISH** son of Sir Woodbine Parish K. C. H., who was born XVIth Dec: mdcccxxxiii and died xxiiird Sept: mcmiv, Vicar of Selmeston cum Alciston and Chancellor of Chichester Cathedral his surviving brothers and sister dedicate this window.

Stained glass window. LH side: kneeling figure of a crowned and sainted bishop below two angels. Scrolls appear to read 'Ave Maria grapla' and 'Dominus tecu'. RH side: kneeling female figure, probably Mary, with white lilies. She is beneath two angels. Scroll reads 'Ecce ancilla Domini' (Behold the handmaid of the Lord) and a book is open at the word 'Exultavi' (I rejoiced). The design is very detailed, & signed in the bottom left hand corner with a small wheatsheaf, the signature of Charles Kempe. There is a boxed text in the bottom right hand corner. Parish was born in 1833 and died in 1904.

See also A17 and J08. Burial on 27 September 1904, aged 70, presided over by Robert Sutton, Archdeacon of Lewes (PR).

Plot J04   BRAY

Frieze

: QUIDQUID : AGAS : OMNIA : ~
: IN : GLIAS: DEI : FACITO : ~

On back of recess

HER LYETH DAM BETRIS BRAY ~
SUMTYME THE WYFFE OF SUR
EDWARD BRAY & DAWGTER OF
RAFFE SHERLEY OF WYSTON ~
& WYFE OF EDWARD ELDERTON
VERMIB - - - - CESI SAXO HOC
SIGNATA BEATRIS AT SECUNDUS
R- -   - - ACS- -

HERE LYETH DAME **BEATRICE BRAY**
SOMTIME THE WIFE OF SIR
EDWARD BRAY AND DAUGHTER OF
RALPH SHERLEY OF WISTON
& WIFE OF EDWARD ELDERTON
WORMS. . . . .

Edge of chest lid

VOS MIHI DEFUNCTE VIVI IMPLORATE SALUTEM ~
FLECTINAMQUE PIANVMINAMENTE VOLUTAT

Stone chest tomb set into the north wall of the chancel. The lower
part of the monument is a chest tomb with four quatrefoils carved
into the front, each containing a different stylized flower. Above is a
recess roofed by a 'Tudor' arch. Graffiti on the back include a
windmill and a two-storey house with leaning chimney. The house is
carved in 'wrigglework', with lines in a distinctive zig-zag. Fluted
pilasters on each side are topped by capitals. There is a frieze of
leaves and berries along the level top. There are carved, incised
inscriptions along the frieze and along the edge of the chest lid. The
lettering is eccentric, so the Latin recorded above is only an
approximation. Nairn & Pevsner (1965) describe the tomb as 'an
Easter Sepulchre, a recess with a depressed almost straight arch
and a cresting'. Beatrice Bray died in 1532. William Parish recorded
the inscription as headed with that date, and recorded it as follows;

continued

> 1532
> Here lyeth Dam Betris Bray
> sumtym the wyffe of Sir Edward Bray
> and Daugter of Raffe Shirley
> of Wyston and wyffe of
> Edward Elderton
>
> Vermibus esca jaces saxo hoc signata Beatrix.
> Quicquid agas omnia in gloriam Dei facito.
> Vos mihi defunctae vivi implorate salutem
> Flectinamque pia numina mente voluat.

Plot J05   ?

- - -

Brass plate attached to east wall of chancel with Bible quotation
from Exodus I – V.

Plot J06   BILLITER

Left hand side.
> I believe in God the Father . . . [The Creed]

Right hand side
> Our Father . . . [The Lord's Prayer]

Bottom RH corner
> To the Glory of God:
> the gift of Madam **MARY BILLITER**
> of the Manor of Sherrington.
> 1881

Brass plate attached to east wall of chancel above the altar.
Inscription divided into two halves, left and right. Extra small plate
added in bottom right hand corner.

Plot J06A   **MATTHEWS**

In Loving Memory of
KATHLEEN MAY MATTHEWS
died 25th August 1988
aged 84 years
One Time Verger
of This Church

Wooden cross on the altar with small brass plate on its side.

Plot J07   **?**

- - -

Brass plate attached to east wall of chancel. Bible quotation from
Exodus Chapter XX, Verses 5-10.

Plot J08   **PARISH**

In memory of
WILLIAM DOUGLAS PARISH,
born 1833: died 1904:
Vicar of Selmeston-cum-Alciston from 1863 to 1904
and Chancellor of Chichester Cathedral
1877 to 1900:
this memorial was erected by his loving Parishioners.

Brass plate mounted on red-marble plaque. The brass plate has an
elaborate foliate border. Incised black-painted lettering; the initial
capitals were originally painted red.

Plot J09	CALDICOT

MATTHIAS CALDICOT
of Sherrington Gent
Died Feb^ry 2.AD.
1719. Aet. 65.

Rectangular white marble slab in the floor. Carved arms in roundel at top. Incised lettering. Arms incomplete? Three leopards at top and 2 blank spaces below. Low tablet in white stone standing on white rectangular stone base, with pot-stand behind. The A of Caldicot was originally an O, later corrected to A. Buried 13 February (PR).

Plot J10	SKINNER

Cross

IHS enclosed in quatrefoil at the crossing.
Trinity diagram at the foot:
P (Patris) in circle at top,
F (Filius) in circle lower right,
SS (Spiritu Sanctu) in circle on left.
These three are connected by the label 'non est'
DEUS in the circle at the centre,
linked with the other three circles by radial labels 'est'

Rectangle below

In Affectionate Remembrance.

Top

MARY wife of James **SKINNER**, Esqr of Sherrington
of this Parish, died September 1819, aged 26 years.

Left

CATHERINE daughter of James and Mary
SKINNER, died Augt 1819, aged 5 years.

Right

SARAH ANN daughter of James and Mary
SKINNER, died Oct 26th 1837, aged 21 years.

continued

Bottom

JAMES SKINNER Esqr of Sherington in this
Parish, died November 5. 1873, Aged 88.

Rectangular black Purbeck Marble slab with brass cross inset and
brass border. Black painted incised lettering. Mary was from
Alfriston (PR). The diagram is a visual explanation of one of the
great enigmas of Christianity, the Holy Trinity. Jesus, the Son, is not
the Father, nor is he the Holy Spirit, but all three are God.

Plot J11	RUMSLEY

+

REUBEN RUMSLEY,
50 years Parish Clerk,
Died 1863,
Aged 79.

Diamond shaped brass plate in floor. Black incised lettering, red
cross at top. Buried 12 July 1863 (PR).

Plot J12	RUMSLEY

JOHN RUMSLEY.
Parish Clerk 41 Years.
1828 – 1918.

Diamond shaped brass plate in floor. Buried 26 January <u>1916</u> (PR)

Plot J13	WOODHAMS

+

FANNIE KATE died 1857,
EDWARD SWAN died 1859,
+ **RHODA** died 1864, +
Infant Children of
George and Frances
WOODHAMS.

+

continued

Diamond shaped brass plate in floor. Four red crosses, one in each corner. Fannie buried 7 May 1857, aged 1 year and 3 months. Edward buried 28 January 1859, aged 1 year and 4 months. Rhoda buried 17 August 1864, aged 1 day (PR).

Plot J14   MATTHEWS

+

**ALFRED
MATTHEWS**
50 years Verger
of this Church
1878 - 1954

Diamond shaped brass plate in floor. Red cross at top. Buried 29 January 1954, aged 76 years (PR).

Plot J15   RUMSLEY

+

HARRIET
widow of
Reuben **RUMSLEY**
died 1867
aged 76.

+

Diamond shaped brass plate in floor. Red cross at top and bottom. Buried 14 February 1867 (PR). See H16.

Plot J16   RUMSLEY

+

EMILY RUMSLEY
widow of
John Rumsley
died 1921
aged 89

continued

Diamond shaped brass plate in floor. Black cross at top. Buried 26 May 1921 (PR). See H12.

Plot J16A   WOODHAMS

+
**CHARLOTTE
WOODHAMS**
died 1871
Aged 16
months

Small red tile in the centre of the group of six small diamond-shaped brass plates in the floor. Charlotte lived at Arlington and was buried 1 March 1871 (PR).

Plot J17   HOCKHAM

+
ANNE HOCKHAM,
died Dec 21st 1856,
aged 68.
+
Diamond shaped brass plate in floor. Red crosses top and bottom.

Plot J18   AVIS

+
WILLIAM
died 1851
aged 9 years,
RUTH died 1851 aged 5 years,
ALBERT died 1857 aged 4 years,

continued

Children of
Richard and Sophia
AVIS
+

Diamond shaped brass plate in floor. Black lettering with red capitals. Black crosses top and bottom. Ruth buried 19 August 1851. Albert buried 9 December 1857, aged 3 years and 10 months (PR).

Plot J19   **HOCKHAM**

+
RUTH HOCKHAM,
born June 6th 1818,
died Oct. 30th 1848
aged 50.
+

Diamond shaped brass plate in floor. Black crosses top and bottom. See E01.

Plot J20   **MARCHANT**
Given by his family in memory of
WALTER MARCHANT who was organist here
for 60 years he was also Churchwarden
and tended the Churchyard for much
of that time. 26 – 7 – 1899 to 18 – 10 – 1988

Reader's desk with small brass plate facing aisle. Walter lived at Church Farm, Selmeston; buried 24 October 1988, aged 89 years (PR).
The organ came from St Andrew's Church in Norway, Eastbourne, when S. F. Morgan was vicar. Mr H. Davis, the local joiner, made a new case for it, and fitted pedals with wider-than-usual spacing. Walter Marchant, who was organist from 1919 until 1979, always played the organ in his boots. See B33.

Plot J21   **CALDICOTT**

Near this place are buried **MATTHIAS CALDICOTT** of Sherrington in this Parish who died 1719 and **KATHERINE** his wife died 1743 Also their children **MATTHIAS** d. 1723 **WILLIAM** d. 1719 **KATHERINE** d 1772 **LEONARD** d. 1686 **GEORGE** born 1688 **ANN** born 1690 **ELIZABETH** d. 1766 **SAMUEL** d. 1772

Long brass plate running along the altar step and facing west. Black lettering with capitals in red. Matthias buried 13 February 1720, affidavit receiving. Catherine buried 4 February 1744. Matthias buried 10 March 1724. William buried 11 June 1719. Catherine buried 20 June 1772, infant. Leonard buried 31 December 1686 'in woollen'. 'Miss Elizabeth' buried 31 May 1766. Samuel buried 24 February 1772, gent (PR).

Plot J22   **DINNIS**

THOMAS HENRY DINNIS
1916 – 1983 lived and farmed
in this Parish for 42 years
a gentle and much loved man

Grey marble plaque mounted on wall. Incised red painted lettering.

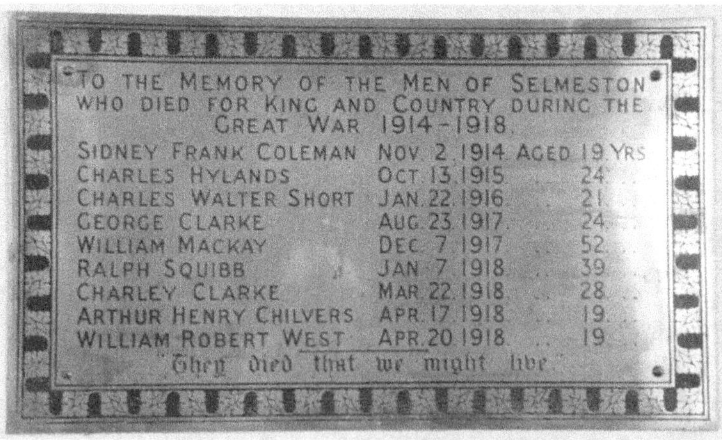

Plot J23   WAR MEMORIAL

To the Memory of the Men of Selmeston
who died for King and Country during the
Great War 1914 – 1918

SIDNEY FRANK COLEMAN Nov. 2. 1914. aged 19. yrs.
CHARLES HYLANDS Oct. 13. 1915. aged 24. yrs.
CHARLES WALTER SHORT Jan. 22. 1916. aged 21. yrs.
GEORGE CLARKE Aug. 23. 1917. aged 24. yrs.
WILLIAM MACKAY Dec. 7. 1917. aged 52. yrs.
RALPH SQUIBB Jan. 7. 1918. aged 39. yrs.
CHARLEY CLARKE Mar. 22. 1918. aged 28. yrs.
ARTHUR HENRY CHILVERS Apr. 17. 1918. aged 19. yrs.
WILLIAM ROBERT WEST Apr. 20. 1918. aged 19. yrs.

- - -

"They died that we might live."

Brass war memorial plate attached to wall. Decorative border.
Similar in style to the equivalent memorial in Alciston Church. See
Appendix B.

Plot J24   ROGERS

The body of **HENRY ROGERS**
a painefvll preacher · in · this chvrch two
and thirty · yeeres · who dyed the sixt of
May anodni 1639 and in the yeere
of · his · age · 67 · lyeth · heere · expecting ·
the · second coming of ovr lord
· Iesus Christ ~
I · did · beleeve · and therefore spake.
Whereof · I taught I doe pertake. –
HENRY ROGERS.

continued

Rectangular brass plaque in the floor of the south aisle. Incised and black painted lettering. Spaces between words initially lightly marked with faint crosses. Some of these were later turned into dots with a punch, but not all, implying that the job was not properly finished. Described by Davidson-Houston in 1938 (SAC 79, 74-130) as 'seventeen and one-eighth inches by seven and one-quarter inches with seven lines in Roman capitals and two English verses'. He noted that the inscription was the wrong way up, but since then it has been corrected. The addition of Henry Rogers' name at the end is unusual; it looks almost like a signature, which it surely cannot be. Henry Rogers was vicar of Selmeston 1607-1639. 'Painefull' meant 'painstaking'; 'anodni' meant 'anno domini'.

Plot J25   MOCKETT
Centre

+

MARTHA
the wife of
George **MOCKETT**
died Oct. 25,
1873,
aged 63.

+

Round the sides

Jesus said / she is not /
dead but / sleepeth

Diamond shaped brass plaque in floor.

Plot J26   GUY

+

MARY
Wife of
John **GUY,**
died 29. Feby 1868
aged 65

+

Diamond shaped brass plaque in floor. Red crosses above and below. Black lettering, capitals in red.

Plot J27   **RUMSLEY**

+

**ADA
EMILY RUMSLEY,**
born Aug. 10. 1868,
died May 28,
1870.

+

Diamond shaped brass plaque in floor. Crosses above and below.
Black lettering, capitals in red.

Plot J28   **RICHARDSON**

+

**THOMAS
RICHARDSON**
died1866
aged 27 years

+

Diamond shaped brass plaque in floor. Crosses above and below.
Thomas's last address Brighton. Buried 14 February 1866 (PR).

Plot J29   **POTTER**

+

MYRA JANE POTTER,
died 5th June 1877,
aged 19 years.

+

Diamond shaped brass plaque in floor. Crosses above and below.

Plot J30 POTTER

JAMES
POTTER
died 1871,
Aged 14
years.
+

Diamond shaped brass plaque in floor. Cross below, no cross above.
Buried 14 April 1871 (PR).

Plot J31 POTTER

ANN
POTTER
died 1865.
Aged 4
years.
+

Diamond shaped brass plaque in floor. No cross above, cross below.
Anne, with an 'e', was buried 26 November 1865 (PR).

Plot J32 POTTER

+
KATE POTTER
died 20th March
1874,
aged 3 years.
+

Diamond shaped brass plaque in floor. Crosses above and below.

Plot J33   LATHAM
Border

In affectionate memory of
HENRY LATHAM Vicar of Selmeston died 1866.

And **MARIA** his wife died 1846
placed here by a few friends and parishioners.

Miniature version of J10. Rectangular black marble slab with brass cross and border. The cross has 'IHS' at the crossing. Henry died of cholera in Boulogne. Maria buried 8 September 1846, aged 50 (PR). Henry buried in Boulogne?

Plot J34   HOCKHAM

+

**WILLIAM
HOCKHAM,**
died 1871,
aged 55.

+

Diamond shaped brass plaque in floor. Crosses above and below. William's last address was West Firle Union. Buried 26 August 1871.

Plot J35   HOCKHAM

+

**JAMES
HOCKHAM**
died Aug. 10. 1869,
aged 41.

+

Diamond shaped brass plaque in floor. Lettering painted black, with red capitals. Crosses above and below. Lived at Milton Street (PR).

Plot J36   MOCKETT

+

JOHN
FENNELL
~ son of ~
Henry and Hetty
MOCKETT.
died1848.
aged 27.

+

Diamond shaped brass plaque in floor. Crosses above and below. Like his parents, John lived at Firle; buried 21 June 1848 (PR). See A06.

Plot J37   MOCKETT

+

ANN,
Wife of
Henry **MOCKETT.**
died 1796.
aged 26.

+

Diamond shaped brass plaque in floor. Crosses painted red above and below. Anne was buried 2 November 1796 (PR). See A06

Plot J38   MOCKETT

+

HETTY,
Wife of
Henry **MOCKETT.**
died 1841.
aged 63.

Diamond shaped brass plaque in floor. Crosses above and below. Hetty was buried 17 August 1841 (PR). See A06.

Plot J39   **MOCKETT**

+

HENRY MOCKETT.
died 1853,
aged 78.

+

Diamond shaped brass plaque in floor. Red crosses above and
below. Henry buried 6 January 1853, aged 79 (PR). See A06.

Plot J40   **COX**
Top

ANN, Widow of William **COX**, of Stanstead
in the County of Kent

+

and daughter of

RH side

Robert and Elizabeth Rochester.

LH side

Died 1741, aged 57 years.

Large Purbeck marble slab with brass borders. Marble bears a large
coat of arms carved in high relief. Brass borders bear the
inscription.
Ann was buried 3 December 1741 (PR).

Plot J41   **SKINNER**

This window was erected by the Friends of **JAMES SKINNER Esq**re
of Sherrington in this Parish, in thankful remembrance of many
mercies received through his instrumentality. AD 1867. Ecclesiasticus
III VIII.1.

continued

<table>
<tr><td>

Long brass plate on north wall under window. Lettering in relief, with red paint on the capitals. Decorative quatrefoil at the end of the inscription. The biblical reference, Ecclesiasticus 38.1, is 'Honour a physician with the honour due unto him for the uses ye may have of him: for the Lord hath created him.' James Skinner was a doctor; hence the punning use of the word 'instrumentality'. See G03 and J10.

</td></tr>
</table>

<table>
<tr><td>

Plot J42　　　　　　　　　　　　　　　　　　　　　　　**HARBER**

Centre

+

JANE HARBER,

+　　died August 30th 1884,　　+

aged 49 years.

+

Edges

+ Watch · therefore +

+ for · ye · know · not +

+ what · hour · your +

+ Lord · doth · come +

Red speckled marble. Diamond-shaped plaque set in floor. Cross in each corner. Lettering painted in black, with capitals in red. Jane lived at Firle (PR).

</td></tr>
</table>

<table>
<tr><td>

Plot J43　　　　　　　　　　　　　　**BALCOMBE/ TEELING**

+

WILLIAM BALCOMBE,

born May 19 1799, died

13 December 1876, aged 77 years.

CAROLINE BALCOMBE, born April 11 1793,

died 10 February 1863, aged 70 years,

continued

</td></tr>
</table>

THOMAS BALCOMBE, born Sep. 22 1827,
died Oct. 28 1852, aged 25 years.

MARIA MARGARET TEELING,
died Sep. 7 1849,
aged 17 years,
+

Diamond shaped brass plaque in floor. Red crosses above and below.
The name 'Balcombe' spelt 'Balcomb' in PR.

Plot J44   GUTSELL/ PIERCE
+
In memory of
LEVI GUTSELL,
died 1 Feb. 1860,
aged 65, and
MARY his wife, died 31 July 1858, aged 71;

Also of her daughter **MARY ANN** wife of
David Pierce of Cobb Court in this Parish,
~ died 8 Feb. 1874, aged 54: ~

And of **GEORGE PIERCE** son of
David and Mary Ann Pearce,
died June 3 1840,
Aged 18 months.
+

Diamond shaped brass plaque in floor. Red crosses above and below.
Mary Ann's and George Frederick's surname spelt Pearce in PR.

<table>
<tr><td>

Plot J45

</td><td align="right">

?

</td></tr>
</table>

Here lieth interr'd
The remains of **ELIZ[ABETH]**
- - - - Daughter of
- - - - -   - - - - - - Gent
and - - - - - - Wife
[who departed this] life

- - - - - -

Aged - - Years

Also of - - - - - - -
their? youngest Daughter
Who departed this life

- - - -

Aged - - Years

Rectangular pale stone slab in floor. Not in its original position, in the floor of the church, but relaid in the vestry during the rebuilding. Badly damaged incised inscription.

<table>
<tr><td>

Plot J46

</td><td align="right">

?

</td></tr>
</table>

Illegible inscription

Rectangular slab in floor. Not in its original position, which was in the floor of the church, but relaid in the vestry during the rebuilding. The inscription has been worn to the point of illegibility. A cupboard covers part of the stone.

Plot J47   ROCHESTER

Near this Tomb lye inter'd the Bodys of
HENRY
ROCHESTER late of this
parish deceased and **SUSANNA** his
wife who was the Daughter of
William Markwick of Wannock
in the parish of Lavington Ese [?] deceased.
The said Henry departed this Life
the 10th day of September 1703 Aged 45.
And the said Susanna the 23rd day
of May 1726 Aged 78.

Rectangular black slab in floor. Not in its original position, in the floor of the church, but relaid in the vestry during the rebuilding.

Plot J48   ROCHESTER

Apostrophe ad
omnes
This life that's packt with jelousies & fears
I love not that's beyond ye lists of tears
That life for me foe here I cannot breath
My prayers out there I shall have wreath
To say Our Father that's in heaven wth me
Where chores of Sancts & Innocents there be
Christianos
No sooner Christned but possession
I took of heavenlie habitation

Here Lyeth ye body of
HENRYROCHESTER
dyed May 28 1646
-

continued

Our suggested reading, though not the only possible reading,
runs as follows:

Address to
everyone.
This life, that's packed with jealousies and fears,
I love not. That's beyond the lists of tears,
That life for me; for here I cannot breathe
My prayers out. There I shall have breath
To say 'Our Father that's in Heaven'. With me
Were choirs of saints and innocents. There be
Christianos.
No sooner christened, but possession
I took of heavenly habitation.
Here lies the body
of Henry Rochester,
died May 28, 1646.

Another reading, by Thomas Horsfield Vol 2, p 334:

Apostrophe ad omnes.
This life, that's packt with jelousies and fears,
I love not: that's beyond the list of tears,
That life for me: for here I cannot wreath
To say yur Father that's in heaven with me,
Where chores of sancts and innocents there be.
Christianos.
No sooner christen'd, but possession
I took of th' heavenlie habitation.

Rectangular black slab in floor. Not in its original position, in the
floor of the church, but relaid in the vestry during the rebuilding.
The second part of the enigmatic inscription is carved, unusually, at
right angles to the first part. Nothing to help us in the surviving PR.

Plot J49   **ROCHESTER**

Intered ye body of
Mrs ELIZABETH ROCHESTER
widow of Robert
Rochester late of
Ludlay Gent Who
Departed this [Life]
Ye 13th day of M—
Aged 77 years M[other?]
of the above said Mary

Rectangular slab of pale stone set in floor. Not in its original position, in the floor of the church, but relaid in the vestry during the rebuilding. In 1834, 'Three large slabs of marble record the names, ages, and deaths, of several members connected with the ancient family of Rochester.' [Horsfield Vol 2, p 334]

~

~ End Notes ~

ESRO = East Sussex Record Office

Chapter 1: Acknowledgments & Introduction
1. Seaford Monumental Inscriptions Group 2013 and 2014; Castleden & Murray 2016 and 2018.
2. Horsfield, I, 333-334.
3. The Caldicott family was not by any means ancient (see Chapter 4): nor, by 1832, was it very respectable (see Chapter 5).
4. Mary and Sarah Skinner have a memorial at Selmeston: J10.
5. There are Rochester memorials at Selmeston: J40, J47, J48, J49.
6. Revd John Nutt, Rector of Berwick who lived at Mays in Selmeston, is buried at Berwick (see K12 and K22 in the Berwick monumental inscriptions volume).
7. Allodial means that the holder of the land was exempt from feudal duties.

Part One
Church & Churchyard: A Long History

Chapter 2: Very early beginnings: no bustle at all
1. Not 'between 1000 and 5000 BC' as described in the Draft Conservation Area Character Appraisal.
2. Harris 2007.
3. Holloway 1979.
4. Margary 1955.
5. Sussex Archaeological Collections 13, 55.
6. Margary 1939; Patent Roll 37 Henry III, m.6.
7. Margary 1939.

Chapter 3: Selmeston in the Dark Ages

1. The ancient cemetery's grid reference is TQ 510070.
2. Welch 1983, II, 389-90.
3. Welch 1971; Welch 1983.
4. Castleden 2019, 183-86; Anon 2019 Draft Conservation Area Character Appraisal.
5. Welch 1983, II, 390-1.

Chapter 4: Medieval and Early Modern Selmeston

1. Sawyers 1887. In his *Dictionary of the Sussex Dialect*, Revd William Parish published a crisp warning regarding the problems surrounding derivations of words, 'not only on account of the prevalence and perpetuation of erroneous derivations already existing, on the authority of persons who knew nothing whatever of the subject, but also because there are so few works published on the subject which are reliable.' (Parish 1875, 3)
2. Poole 1948.
3. Castleden 2019, 116; 145; 161-64; 171-73; 221-27.
4. Baxter 1836.
5. Baxter 1836.
6. www.dorsetcountymuseum.org
7. Barker 1990.
8. Godman 1911.
9. ESRO: SAS/P 461. The grant is dated 27 November 1533. Sir Edward's deceased wife is referred to as 'Lady Beatrice'. We have been unable to find out where The Krinkk was, or what the word means. The plot does not appear on the Tithe Map.
10. W. D. C. 1867.
11. Banks & Turner 1886.
12. Merrifield 1950.
13. ESRO: PAR 482/7/9/2. George de Paris's paintings of Selmeston church are listed in *Catalogue of One Thousand Original Studies in Water Colours*, published in Brighton in 1899, page 34.

Chapter 5: Modern Selmeston

1. And seven more stanzas. The line 'Them that asks no questions' is a typical Kipling vulgarism, the sort of thing that grates with many modern readers.
2. UK Home Office Criminal Petitions; British Convict Transportation Registers 1787-1867.
3. ESRO: PAR 482/7/9/1. The Diana Latham painting is described as 'Watercolour of the church exterior from the NE, including the churchyard.'
4. Anon 1880.
5. Castleden & Murray 2018, 51-72.
6. ESRO: PAR 482/7/9/2. George de Paris's painting of Selmeston church is listed in *Catalogue of One Thousand Original Studies in Water Colours*, published in Brighton in 1899, page 34.
7. Anon 1880.
8. Anon 1880.
9. Anon 1880.
10. The 1890 restoration of St Andrew's, Lyddington, has been described by Simon Jenkins as 'ruthless' and Christian's design for his own house has been condemned as 'his horrible self-inflicted home at Hampstead.'
11. Banks & Turner 1886.
12. Merrifield 1950.
13. ESRO: SAS/G 5/35; W/A 70 233; LT; PAR 230 1/1/3; PAR 482 1/5/1; XA 27/13.
14. I vividly remember similar collapsible wooden pews existing in Canterbury Cathedral in the 1950s. It was a favourite haunt of mine as a boy and on one occasion I took my grandmother with me. She accidentally but memorably knocked the folding pews at the back of the nave over during a service. They went over one after another, like dominoes. In the rich and reverberant acoustic of the cathedral, it sounded like heavy gunfire from a battleship. The Battle of Jutland, which took place when my grandmother was 36, must have sounded much

like that. She was mortified. I was surprised we were not asked to leave.

15. ESRO: PAR 482/7/9/3.

16. The upper picture shows the eastern pair of windows, featuring Mary Magdalene on the left carrying a jar; the two women on the right may be Mary and Martha. The centre picture shows the middle pair of windows. This depicts Mary Magdalene on the left visiting the tomb of Jesus on Easter morning and encountering the angel. The image on the right shows the angel sitting on the tomb. The lower picture shows the western pair of windows, depicting the Last Supper. The windows are well composed, tastefully coloured and pleasing to look at, but they do not appear to tell a coherent narrative.

Chapter 6: Through the Looking-Glass

1. *Sussex Daily News* 24 Sep 1904; ESRO PAR 482/7/6/1 Biographical sketch of W. D. Parish.

2. In the introduction to his *Dictionary of the Sussex Dialect*, William Parish gently disparaged the country folk of Sussex in other ways. 'It is surprising,' he wrote, 'how little trouble people will take to ascertain correctly even the names of their neighbours, and I know of an instance of a man who lost sight of his own name altogether, from having been accustomed for many years to hear it mispronounced. But this in a great measure is to be attributed to the fact that a musical ear is very rarely found among Sussex people, a defect which is remarkably shown not only in the monotonous tunes to which their old songs are sung, but also in the songs themselves, which are almost entirely devoid of rhythm.'

3. ESRO: AMS 1009/1015.

~

~ References~

SAC= Sussex Archaeological Collections.

SEAMIG = Seaford Monumental Inscriptions Group.

Anon 1880? The Old Church of Selmeston, Sussex. *Unknown journal* 31, 296-99. [article found in Selmeston Church; photocopied from an untraced journal, with no note of source].

Anon 2019 *Draft Conservation Area Character Appraisal: Selmeston.* Wealden District Council.

Banks, W. and Turner, W. W. 1886 *Seaford: Past and Present. Handbook and Visitors' Guide.*Seaford: Banks.

Barker, K. 1990 The Mizmaze at Leigh. *Caerdroia* 23, 9-14.

Baxter, J. 1836 *Baxter's agricultural and horticultural gleaner, containing important discoveries.* London: Simpkin, Marshall & Co.

Brydges, Sir Egerton 1782 *Topographical Miscellanies, containing ancient histories and modern descriptions of mansions, churches, monuments and families, with many engravings, particularly of ancient architecture, throughout England.* Vol 1. London: Robson and Symonds.

Castleden, R. 2019 *Ancient Seaford: Ice Age to Norman Conquest.* Seaford: Blatchington Press.

Castleden, R. and Murray, A. 2016 *All is Hush'd: Bishopstone Church & Churchyard.* Seaford: Blatchington Press.

Castleden, R. and Murray, A. 2018 *Go home, dear friends: Berwick Church & Churchyard.* Seaford: Blatchington Press.

Curwen, E. and Curwen, E. C. 1938 Late Bronze Age ditches at Selmeston. *SAC* 79, 195-98.

Davidson-Houston, C. E. D. 1938 Sussex monumental brasses. *SAC* 79, 74-130.

Godman, P. S. 1911 On a series of rolls of the manor of Wiston. *SAC* 56, 130-82.

Harris, R. B. 2005 *Ditchling Historic Character Assessment Report.*

Sussex Extensive Urban Survey (EUS).

Holloway, A. E. 1979 An excavation at Selmeston, East Sussex, 1978. *SAC* 117, 240-247.

Horsfield, T. 1834 *The History, Antiquities and Topography of the County of Sussex*. Lewes: Baxter.

Margary, I. D. 1939 Roman roads from Pevensey to Firle and Glynde, and to the Downs by Wannock. *SAC* 80, 29-61.

Margary, I. D. 1940 Roman centuriation at Ripe. *SAC* 81, 31-41.

Margary, I. D. 1955 Roman Roads in Britain.

Mee, A. 1937 *Sussex: the garden by the sea*. London: Hodder & Stoughton.

Merrifield, R. 1950 Good Friday customs in Sussex. *SAC* 89, 85-97.

Nairn, I. and Pevsner, N. 1965 *The buildings of England: Sussex*. Harmondsworth: Penguin Books.

Parish, Revd W. D. 1875 *A dictionary of the Sussex dialect and collection of provincialisms in use in the County of Sussex*. Lewes: Farncombe & Co.

Poole, H. 1948 The Domesday Book churches of Sussex. *SAC* 87, 29-76.

Renshaw, W. C. 1912 Some clergy of the archdeaconry of Lewes and South Malling Deanery. *SAC* 55, 220-277.

Rudling, D. 1985 Recent archaeological research at Selmeston, East Sussex. *SAC* 123, 1-25

Sawyers, F. E. 1887 Glossary of Sussex dialectal place-nomen-clature. *SAC* 35, 165-172.

SEAMIG 2013 *As I am now, so you must be: Monumental Inscriptions at St Peter's, East Blatchington*. Seaford: Blatchington Press.

SEAMIG 2014 *Testimony of Regard: Monumental Inscriptions at St Leonard's, Seaford*. Seaford: Blatchington Press.

Stimpson, F. 2016 Reading Gilbert White: W. D. Parish's annotations of *The Natural History of Selborne*. SAC 154, 243-56.

Torr, V. J. B. 1920 An Elizabethan return of the state of the Diocese of Chichester. *SAC* 61, 92-124.

W. D. C. 1867 Valuation of the Rapes of Lewes and Pevensey,

1649. *SAC* 19, 207-8.

Welch, M. G. 1971 Late Romans and Saxons in Sussex. *Britannia* 2, 232-37.

Welch, M G. 1980 The Saxon cemeteries of Sussex, in Rahtz, P., Dickinson, T. and Watts, L. (ed) *Anglo-Saxon Cemeteries 1979*, pp 255-83.

Welch, M. G. 1983 Early Anglo-Saxon Sussex. *British Archaeological Reports Series* 112, Parts 1 and 2 (2 volumes).

Whitley, H. M. 1920 Sanctuary in Sussex. *SAC* 61, 80-91.

~

~ Appendix A ~

Vicars of Selmeston

Parish of Selmeston

John Bontynge installed 1350
James Porter installed 1386
John Perot installed 1391
Robert atte More installed 1391
Simon Bridham installed 1400 (exchanged)
John Wykeham installed 1400
Thomas Benet installed 1401
John Amys installed 1402
John Inglewood installed 1411
John Selys installed 1437
Alan Edward installed 1442 (deprived)
Richard Rawden installed 1443
John Whytyington installed 1486
Walter Walwyn installed 1509
Anthony Lyle AM installed 1530
William Saywell installed 1547
John Levett installed 1560, but a review of the state of the diocese in
    1563 noted 'Selmyston having no vicar nor curat.' [Torr 1920]
Robert Parrys installed 1564
Peter Parris installed 1569
Robert Bedell (or Bodle) ordained by William Barlow Bishop of
    Chichester 1564, installed at Selmeston 1581
Henry Rogers MA ordained by Thomas Bickley Bishop of
    Chichester 1595, then curate at St Michael's, Lewes, licensed to
    preach 1605, installed 1607, wife Elizabeth, buried at Selmeston 9
    May 1639 **(J24)** [from Renshaw 1912]
John Wilshaw BA installed 1639, a Royalist vicar deprived of his living
    under the Commonwealth in 1645
Martin Fist installed 1645, a Parliamentarian intruded under the
    Commonwealth
Robert Sybson installed 1653, a Parliamentarian who was allowed to
    keep the living after the Restoration
Thomas Higson installed 1664
Henry Green AM installed 1651

William Green, MA 1681-1710 Graduated from Balliol College, Oxford, BA 1673, ordained by Nathaniel Bishop of Oxford 1673, married at All Saints, Lewes to Elizabeth Read, installed 1681, buried at Selmeston 10 August 1710.

Richard Russell AM installed 1710

Walter Bartelott AM installed 1715

Randolph Parry BA installed 1744

John Lloyd MA installed 1748

John Russell BD installed 1777

George Wilson BD installed 1784

Richard Constable MA installed 1785

Stephen Jenkin BA installed 1801, lived initially at Selmeston, later moved to Salehurst, installing a curate at Selmeston: deterioration of vicarage at this time

Thomas Griffith BA installed 1827

Henry Latham MA born 1795, installed 1833, substantially rebuilt the vicarage, left Selmeston for Fittleworth in 1847 after his wife's death; he himself died of cholera in Boulogne in 1866

United Parish of Selmeston-with-Alciston (created 1847)

Henry Foster MA installed 1847

William Douglas Parish SCL Born 1833, installed 1863 died 23 September 1904, buried at Selmeston **(A24, J03, J08)**

William Ridgeway Nightingale MA installed 1903

Robert Buchanan Dunlop MA installed 1916

Frederick Gerald Finch MA installed 1919

Frank Stanford Morgan MA installed 1923

Thomas John Bullick MA installed 1930, first Selmeston vicar to have a telephone (Ripe 35)

Thomas Sydney Goudge MA installed 1938

Leslie Vernon Peacock   installed 1946

Albert Edward Harris installed 1954

William Gordon Calvert Lee MA born 1898, installed 1956, died 1957 **(H04)**

Arthur Charles Austen MA installed 1958

Alan Fryer Nicholls BA installed 1963

Arthur Tindal Hart DD installed 1966

Kenneth Grace BA installed 1976

Vickery Willis House MA installed 1981

Peter Smith BA installed 1990, left 2001
Peter Michael Blee BA BTh installed 2003

~

~ Appendix B ~
Selmeston's War Dead

Names on War Memorial plaque in Selmeston Church

Arthur Henry Chilvers
Private 27466, 1st Battalion, Wiltshire Regiment. Killed in action on 17 April 1918, aged 19. The son of Frederick and Alice Chilvers of Manor Villas (now The Little Manor), Selmeston. Commemorated on the Tyne Cot Memorial in Belgium, Panels 119-120.

Charley Clarke
Died on 22 March 1918, aged 28.

George Clarke
Died on 23 August 1917, aged 24.

Sidney Frank Coleman
Private K/9923, 2nd Battalion, Royal Sussex Regiment. Born at Arlington. Enlisted at Eastbourne. Killed in action on 2 November 1914, aged 19. Commemorated on the Menin Gate Memorial at Ypres, Panel 120.

Charles Hylands
Private G/210, 6th Battalion, The Buffs, East Kent Regiment. Born at Selmeston. Enlisted at Ramsgate, resided at Berwick. The son of J. H. Hylands of Old Town Cottage. Killed in action aged 24. Commemorated on the Loos Memorial in France, Panel 15-19.

William Mackay
Died on 7 December 1917, aged 52. Parish Register tells us he was buried on 11 December 1917. His addresses are given as Tilton House and 3 The Avenue, Eastbourne.

Charles Walter Short
Gunner 97959, C Battery 47th Brigade Royal Field Artillery. Killed in action 22 January 1916, aged 21. The son of Sidney and Emily Short of Fairchildes Farm, Warlingham, Surrey. Commemorated on Hagle Dump Cemetery near Ypres.

Ralph Squibbs
>Private 320490, 16th Battalion Royal Sussex Regiment. Killed in action on 7 January 1918, aged 39. Buried in Hadria Cemetery, Alexandria. Son of George and Annie Squibb. From Clevedon, Somerset.

William Robert West
>Died on 20 April 1918, aged 19.

Names on the Selmeston and Alciston War Memorial

This rough-hewn granite cross erected in 1923 stands by the roadside at the southern end of The Street. All the names above are listed on it, with the addition of several names of Alciston men, under the dedication 'To the memory of the men of Selmeston and Alciston who fell in the Great War 1914-18'. After the Second World War, two further names were added, under the heading '1939-1945'.

Philip George Boys
>Died 8 December 1918 aged 35. From Alciston.

D. F. Gumbrill
>Lance Corporal G/4800, 11th Battalion Royal Sussex Regiment. Born at Stoneham, enlisted at Eastbourne. Killed in action 20 September 1917. Commemorated on Tyne Cot Memorial in Belgium, Panel 86-88. From Alciston.

George Fears
>Private 17027, 1st/6th Battalion Duke of Wellington's (West Riding) Regiment. Died 11 November 1918, the last day of the First World War. The son of Eli and Caroline Fears of Bo-Peep, Alciston. Buried in Alciston churchyard.

Walter David Foord
>Private G/2592, D Company 8th Battalion Royal Sussex Regiment. Born in Alciston. The son of Daniel and Louisa Ford of Swingate Cottages, Firle. Died of wounds 26 January 1916. Buried in the Meaulte Military Cemetery, Somme, Row B30.

James William Hayward
>Private G/50672, 20th Battalion Middlesex Regiment. Father of James

Hayward of Alciston. Killed in action 4 March 1917.Commemorated on Thiepval Memorial in France, Pier and Face 12D and 13B.

George Mockett
Private 48203, 8th Battalion East Surrey Regiment. The son of George and Mary Mockett of Alciston. Died on 24 October 1918. Buried in Preux-Au-Bois Communal Cemetery, France, Row B8.

Hugh McLaren Stacey
Lieutenant 324582, 141st/7th Battalion Royal East Kent Regiment (The Buffs), attached to Royal Armoured Corps. The son of Hugh and Cecilia Stacey of Alciston. Killed in action 1 March 1945 at Weeze in West Germany, aged 19. Awarded the American Bronze Star. Buried in Rheinberg War Cemetery, 13A 25. There is a marble tablet dedicated to Hugh in Alciston church.

Charles Peter Gowers
Able Seaman (Gunner) D/J76630 Royal Navy. Killed in action at the First Battle of Narvik on 10 April 1940. Charles was serving on HMS *Hunter*, an H Class Destroyer. The *Hunter* was badly damaged by gunfire from German destroyers, then collided with HMS *Hotspur*. The *Hunter* sank in the middle of the fjord with the loss of 110 men. Charles Gowers, the son of Herbert and Annie Gowers and the husband of Annie Gowers of Selmeston, is commemorated on Plymouth Naval Memorial, Panel 37 Column 3.

~

~ Index of Monuments ~

~

<h1 style="text-align:center">~ General Index ~</h1>

~ Blatchington Press Books ~

THE WINFRITH LETTERS
by Rodney Castleden & John Urmson

The story of a collaboration. A series of letters between the co-writers
of *Winfrith* shows how a music drama came into being. A blow by
blow account of a race against time to complete a full-scale stageworthy
music drama in time to celebrate the Millennium at Brixworth Church
in Northamptonshire. Includes the full text of the music drama and
samples of the music.

2014. Royal paperback (155 x 235 mm), 278pp. £12.95. ISBN 978-1-
326-10274-6. Available from the author and lulu.com

THE APPLE OF DISCORD
by Rodney Castleden

A reconstruction of one of the oldest poems in the world – the lost
prequel to the Iliad. This is the first time in two thousand years that
anyone has attempted to restore this ancient epic poem. Using
authentic ancient sources, the reconstructed poem re-creates a vanished
Homeric world, half-history, half-legend – the world of Achilles,
Agamemnon, Helen of Troy and the forgotten hero Palamedes.

2015. Royal paperback (155 x 235 mm), 329pp. £12.95.
ISBN 978-1-291-81413-2. Available from lulu.com

THE BIRD MAN OF BLATCHINGTON
by Rodney Castleden

The diaries of Revd Robert Dennis, who was Rector of St Peter's, East
Blatchington in the middle of the nineteenth century. Robert Dennis
recorded his observations of birds in the Ouse and Cuckmere valleys,
in Blatchington village and along the Chalk cliffs.

2011. Royal paperback (155 x 235 mm), 164pp, 27 black & white
illustrations. ISBN 978-1-4466-1580-0 £8.95 Available from lulu.com.

THE WILMINGTON GIANT:
 the Quest for a Lost Myth   *by Rodney Castleden*

An extended edition of the 1983 book about the enigma of the Long
Man of Wilmington, with many new illustrations.
2012. Royal paperback (155 x 235 mm), 256pp, 96 black & white
illustrations. ISBN 978-1-4717-6887-3. £12.95 Available from the
author and lulu.com

ON BLATCHINGTON HILL:
 History of a Downland Village   *by Rodney Castleden*

The story of East Blatchington from prehistoric times to the present
day, including its struggle to keep its identity while Seaford grows
around it.

2011. Royal paperback (155 x 235 mm), 306pp, 108 black & white
illustrations. ISBN 978-1-4478-5768-6 £12.95 Available from the
author, lulu.com and Seaford Museum.

ON BLATCHINGTON BEACH
  A village and the sea.   *by Rodney Castleden*

The eventful story of East Blatchington's relationship with the sea, including the shifting coastline, shipwrecks, wreckers, smugglers and coastguards, a failed French invasion, the 1795 mutiny, the management of seafront development, and the continuing struggle against the sea.

2013. Royal paperback (155 x 235 mm), 246pp, 94 black & white illustrations. ISBN 978-1-4466-1580-0 £12.95 Available from the author, lulu.com and Seaford Museum.

THE SUSSEX COAST: Land, Sea and
  the Geography of Hope   *by Rodney Castleden*

This landscape history narrates the story of the Sussex coast as an unfolding trialogue among people, land and sea.

2013. Crown quarto paperback (189 x 246 mm), 315pp, 135 black & white illustrations. ISBN 978-1-291-128582-6 £15.95 Available from the author, lulu.com or Seaford Museum.

FORLORN & WIDOWED:
  Seaford in the Napoleonic Wars   *by Rodney Castleden*

Seaford was little more than a village, and its days as a port were really over. The French Wars, 1793-1815, saw Seaford militarized with two batteries, a barracks, a signal station and the last of the Martello Towers. It was a rotten borough, with only a hundred voters sending two Members to Parliament. Elections were noisy, with corruption on a grand scale.

2015. Royal paperback (155 x 235 mm), 205pp, 70 black & white illustrations. ISBN 978-1-326-19473-4 £11.95 Available from the author and lulu.com.

ALL IS HUSH'D:

Bishopstone Church & Churchyard

by Rodney Castleden& Ann Murray

The story of Bishopstone church and its churchyard, with a complete record of all the inscriptions. Includes the remarkable history of the site in early and late Saxon periods, and Bishopstone's special role as the religious centre for the area.

2015. Royal paperback (155 x 235 mm), 360pp, 13 plans, 45 black & white illustrations. ISBN 978-1-326-80188-5 £12.95 Available from the author and lulu.com.

THE FAVOURITE VILLAGE

by James Hurdis

The favourite village of James Hurdis was Bishopstone in Sussex. He was born there in 1763 and became its vicar in the 1790s. His long poem is a sustained nostalgic tribute to the village he loved, as it was – as it had been - in the eighteenth century. This is the first modern edition of the poem, first published in 1810. It includes a biography of James Hurdis and notes on the poem by Rodney Castleden .

2015. Royal paperback (155 x 235 mm), 169pp,26 black & white illustrations £8.95. ISBN 978-0-244-09498-0. Available from Seaford Museum, the author and lulu.com

GO HOME, DEAR FRIENDS:

Berwick Church & Churchyard

by Rodney Castleden& Ann Murray

The story of Berwick church and its churchyard, with a complete record of all the inscriptions. A companion book to *All is Hush'd*, exploring little-known aspects of Berwick's history.

2018. Royal paperback (155 x 235 mm), 242pp, 12 plans, 68 black & white illustrations. ISBN 978-0-244-43371-0 £12.95 Available from the author and lulu.com.

THE SEAFORD AXE HOARD

by Rodney Castleden

One of the biggest hoards of prehistoric stone axes ever found in Britain was discovered in Seaford High Street in 1986. This is its story: how it was discovered and then forgotten – and then rediscovered. What can the stone axes tell us about life in Neolithic Seaford, five thousand years ago?

2015. Royal paperback (155 x 235 mm), 134pp, 66 black & white illustrations. ISBN 978-0-244-66978-2 £8.95 Available from the author and lulu.com.

ANCIENT SEAFORD:
Ice Age to Norman Conquest
by Rodney Castleden

The first half million years of Seaford's story – its prehistory, beginning with the arrival of the first people in Britain. Neolithic people set up a flint tool factory on the site of Seaford. In the bronze age a large cemetery of round barrows spread across eastern Seaford. The iron age saw a hillfort built on Seaford Head. When the Saxons arrived in AD 400, they settled first on Rookery Hill and the Seaford area became the core of the new kingdom of the South Saxons. This wide-ranging and challenging book tells a little-known story and reveals some surprising new insights into Seaford's extraordinary ancient past.

2019. Royal paperback (155 x 235 mm), 328pp, 169 black & white illustrations. ISBN 978-0-244-82198-2 £14.95 Available from the author and lulu.com.

Blatchington Press books are available by post from Rodney Castleden, Rookery Cottage, Blatchington Hill, Seaford, East Sussex BN25 2AJ.

Cheques payable to 'R. Castleden'. To cover postage and packing for one book, please add £3: £2 each for more than one book.

~